laugh out loud

laugh out loud

stories to touch your heart & tickle your funny bone

THOMAS NELSON
Since 1798

NASHVILLE   DALLAS   MEXICO CITY   RIO DE JANEIRO   BEIJING

Published in Nashville, Tennessee, by Thomas Nelson. Thomas Nelson is a registered trademark of Thomas Nelson, Inc.

This manuscript was compiled and prepared by Snapdragon Group℠, Tulsa, Oklahoma.
Managing Editor: Darcie Clemen
Text design: Lori Lynch

Thomas Nelson, Inc., titles may be purchased in bulk for educational, business, fund-raising, or sales promotional use. For information, please e-mail SpecialMarkets@ThomasNelson.com.

Some material reprinted from previously published volumes may have been edited slightly from the original.

Scripture quotations noted MSG are from *The Message* by Eugene H. Peterson. © 1993, 1994, 1995, 1996, 2000. Used by permission of NavPress Publishing Group. All rights reserved.

Library of Congress Cataloging-in-Publication Data

Laugh out loud : stories to touch your heart and tickle your funny bone.
    p. cm.
 Includes bibliographical references and index.
ISBN 978-1-4002-8034-6
 1. Religion—Humor. 2. Conduct of life—Humor.
PN6231.R4L38 2009
 818'.60208—dc22   2008050686

Printed in the United States of America

09 10 11 12 13 RRD 6 5 4

You have to laugh. Laughter is a gift that will get you through the worst of times.

—SHEILA WALSH
Overjoyed!

contents

part one

I've Never Seen Those Kids Before in My Life!
Laughing Out Loud at Our Children

part two

Say Goodnight, Gracie!
Laughing Out Loud at Our Spouses

part three

Dogs, Cats, and Caribou!
Laughing Out Loud at Our Animal Friends

part four

Giggling in the Pews
Laughing Out Loud in Our Churches

part five

On the Road and in the Air
Laughing Out Loud at Our Traveling Adventures

part six

A Mind Is a Terrible Thing to Waste!
Laughing Out Loud at Ourselves

I've Never Seen Those Kids Before in My Life!

Laughing Out Loud at Our Children

Most children threaten at times to run away from home.
This is the only thing that keeps some parents going.

—PHYLLIS DILLER

High Drama at the Bank
· carol kent ·

*I*t was a hot, humid summer day. People were irritable and tired from the heat. My friend Lee was impatiently standing in line at the local bank.

A frazzled woman came up the walk. She was half carrying and half dragging her uncooperative son. He appeared to be about five years old, and he was *not* enjoying the opportunity of accompanying his mother on this trip to town. With the child in tow, the woman finally managed to make her way through the heavy doors at the entrance of the building.

In full view of all the bank patrons, she set her shopping bags down and, with two hands, lifted her son in the air and carried him to one of the chairs in the waiting area. Exasperated, she plunked him down on the seat as she spoke in a voice that was audible to all: "I have *had it* with you today! I am *never* taking you shopping with me again! Don't you dare *move* until I come back to this spot! Do you understand me?"

The boy was startled enough to take her seriously. He nodded through his tears. All eyes in the bank were on the child as he whimpered, "But, Mom, *you broke my*—!"

The bank patrons looked aghast! Had this mean mother been so rough on her child that she slammed him into the chair hard enough to cause physical damage? What kind of child abuser was she? Visual daggers were shot in her direction from all parts of the lobby.

At that moment, to the surprise of all judgmental onlookers, the rambunctious child dug his hands into his back pockets and pulled out two totally flattened Ping-Pong balls.

—*Detours, Tow Trucks, and Angels in Disguise*

3

Okay You Guys
· kathy peel ·

As we all know, a seventeen-year-old is smarter than anyone within a fifty-mile radius. Ours thinks one of his God-given duties in life is to inform his less-knowledgeable younger brothers about the hazards of living with an aging, mentally deficient mother. The way he sees it, why tell Aggie jokes when we've got Mom around? He taught them to personalize a few of the latest blonde jokes just for me.

"Want to know how you can tell when Mom's been using her computer?" John astutely asked Joel and James. "There's whiteout on the screen."

After recovering from hysteria, Joel chimed in, "Do you know how to make Mom's eyes sparkle?"

"How?" James asked.

"Shine a flashlight in her ears."

"I love it!" John responded as he caught his breath. "Hey, have you ever wondered if all that mousse Mom uses on her hair is seeping into her brain causing premature senility?"

On that one I burst through the swinging door I'd been hiding behind and snapped, "Okay you guys, read my lips. You're all going to boarding school!"

—*Do Plastic Surgeons Take VISA?*

Always end the name of your child with a vowel,
so that when you yell, the name will carry.

—BILL COSBY

Kids today don't realize how easy they have it.
When I was a kid, we actually had to get out of the
car and *open* the garage door.

—JOE HICKMAN

They're Out to Rule the World

· martha bolton ·

The kids are taking over. I'm not talking about all the doctors, policemen, politicians, and attorneys who seem to be getting younger and younger each year. I'm talking about children. Real children. More specifically, toddlers. They could be your nieces and nephews, your grandchildren, your neighbors' kids, or in some cases, even your own children. And sure, they seem innocent enough sitting there in their cribs or on the floor playing quietly with their toys, but it's all a ruse. They have an agenda, they're committed, and they've been outsmarting us for years. Everything they do is to advance their plan to take over the world, and it's high time someone blew their cover.

First, I'm not sure how they did it, but somehow these little rug rats have managed to take over the control of our television sets. Instead of watching our favorite news programs or the History Channel, we find ourselves caving in to their desires and watching SpongeBob and Jimmy Neutron for hours on end. Granted, we do get involved in the programs and even catch ourselves laughing out loud sometimes, but has anyone played their theme songs backward to see if they're sending subliminal messages to the adult world?

"You will let me play ball in your house."

"You will take me to Chuck E. Cheese's."

"You will give me an advance on my inheritance."

"You will let me braid your hair in tiny little braids and paint your toenails fluorescent pink."

Who knows what kind of adult brainwashing is going on during these seemingly innocent children's shows?

Phase Two apparently happened while many of us middle-agers

were taking naps. These innocent-looking children somehow convinced pharmaceutical companies of the need for our medicine bottles to come with childproof caps. Caps, I might add, that only *children* can open. Now on the surface, childproofing medicine bottles probably sounded like a great idea, and I do not doubt for a minute that the staff at the FDA had plenty of reputable data to convince the agency to jump on board with the seemingly beneficial plan. But the FDA wasn't looking into the future and seeing where this action was taking us as a society.

"I need my heart medication, Joey," Grandpa says. "Can you come over here and get this blasted thing open for me?"

"Sure, Gramps, as soon as you reveal the password to your safety deposit box."

These children are the same ones who also hide our glasses, car keys, wallets, TV Guide, and then merely giggle, clam up, or speak some kind of gibberish when we try to interrogate them about the missing items.

"Where are my keys, Bobby?"

"Ahgagoga."

"Come on, boy, tell Nana where you put them."

"Dimofogu."

Their resistance to these inquisitions would impress military experts worldwide. Both the FBI and CIA have tried to decipher their secret code, but it's unbreakable.

We're headed for trouble, people.

And who is it that gets the power seat at the dinner table? The "high" chair? (See, even the name sounds commanding.) Who is responsible for that incessant pounding on the metal trays that would make even the toughest grandparent shout out every password to every account he's ever owned? These toddlers, that's who.

Remember the good ol' days when children used to be at the mercy of adults when it came to their mobility? They either rode in a stroller or we carried them. That, too, has changed. These days, kids have their own battery-operated cars to putt around in. They're eighteen months old, and already they know how to drive. What's worse, we're probably the ones they persuaded to buy these vehicles for them.

Which brings us to their incredible business sense. These youngsters are nothing short of financial geniuses. Think about it. They come to our houses selling candy for their schools and youth organizations, then they return on Halloween and take it all back! Has anyone done the math on this?

I'm telling you, world, their hostile takeover has been planned right under our noses, and we've been too blinded by their cuteness to see it. They've been holding high-level security meetings in sandboxes all over the globe. Sure, it all looks like innocent play to us, but it isn't. It's their version of Camp David. Why do you think there's always one child who holds that ear-piercing, high-pitched scream? You think it's a tantrum? I used to think that, too.

These toddlers have their own cell phones, computers, playhouses, and miniature emergency vehicles. What do they need us big people for? They've got almost everything required to run the world on their own.

The most amazing thing about this is how these little ones have managed to get us to run their publicity campaigns for them, and we've been doing it pro bono.

"You wanna see some pictures of the most beautiful grandchild on earth?"

"You think she's beautiful, wait 'til you see *my* grandbaby!"

All things considered, maybe we're just getting what we deserve. These little ones have been outsmarting us for years, manipulating us with their cute smiles and endearing hugs, while we've merely sat by and allowed it all to happen.

But it's not too late. No matter how cute they are, we cannot continue to roll over and let these kids take over. We can't bury our heads and pretend we don't know what they're up to. It's time we let them know once and for all who's in charge here! It's time we—

Sorry. I had more to say, but a two-year-old in my doctor's waiting room just took my glasses and won't give them back, so I can't see my laptop keys. And so the conspiracy continues . . .

—*Cooking with Hot Flashes*

An octogenarian was interviewed by a local newspaper
reporter. "Do you have a lot of great-grandchildren?"
the reporter asked.

"To tell the truth," confessed the matriarch,
"I expect they're all pretty ordinary."

—AUTHOR UNKNOWN

Never raise your hand to your children;
it leaves your midsection unprotected.

—ROBERT ORBEN

If I've told the kids once, I've told them a hundred times, "Don't give the dog a bath in the dishwasher!" I have to admit, though, he *does* come out virtually spotless.

—JOE HICKMAN

Insanity is hereditary: You can get it from your children.

—SAM LEVINSON

K. C. and the Ark

· carol kent ·

We headed for Sunday school. My sister Joy and her family were visiting us for the weekend, and we bundled the kids up and jumped into the car. My nephew K. C. was in kindergarten and, when we got to church, he decided he was brave enough to visit the class for his age group, even though he didn't know anybody in Aunt Carol's church. I was relieved to find out my good friend Marilyn would be his teacher. I knew K. C. would be in good hands.

An hour later the Sunday school classes were dismissed, and we picked up K. C. Later, as we stood in the lobby following the church service, Marilyn tapped on my shoulder and whispered, "Does your nephew live on a farm?" I was surprised by the question.

"Yes," I said. "My sister and her husband are renting a little farm and felt it would be good experience for the children to raise a couple of goats and some chickens. K. C. has daily chores with the animals. Why do you ask?"

Marilyn smiled. "I thought so," she said.

Marilyn had been teaching the story of Noah's ark. She painstakingly explained to the children how large the ark was and that two of every kind of animal got on this big boat before the Great Flood. Then she explained how long they were on the ark before they landed on top of Mount Ararat.

K. C.'s eyes got bigger and bigger. As Marilyn finished the story, she asked, "Does anybody have a question?"

K. C.'s hand shot up in the air. Fresh from his personal experience with animals and farm chores, he did have a question! "Teacher," he said intensely, "what I want to know is who had to clean up all that poop?"

A good question!

—*Detours, Tow Trucks, and Angels in Disguise*

Fascinating Wisdom I Learned from Noah and His Ark

· author unknown ·

1. Don't miss the boat.
2. Don't forget that we're all in the same boat.
3. Plan ahead. It wasn't raining when Noah built the ark.
4. Stay fit. When you're 600 years old, someone might ask you to do something REALLY BIG.
5. Don't listen to critics; just get on with what has to be done.
6. Build your future on high ground.
7. For safety's sake, travel in pairs.
8. Speed isn't always an advantage; the snails were on board with the cheetahs.
9. When you're stressed, float awhile.
10. Remember that the ark was built by amateurs, and the Titanic was built by professionals.
11. No matter the storm, when you're with God there's a rainbow waiting.
12. Remember that woodpeckers inside are more of a threat than the storm outside.

College-Bound Kids Empty Our Nest

· marti attoun ·

With two kids moving into college dorms, I'm feeling weepy and looking as pathetic as the "Homeless Pet of the Week."

It's not empty-nest syndrome. It's the larval stage of another affliction: plundered-nest syndrome. My daughter packed up the only hair dryer, hair curlers, and hand mirror in the house. I have a unibrow, but no tweezers. I have a bleak pallor, but no blush.

Every time I look around, I miss my grown-up kids—or my alarm clock, spare hangers, AA batteries, calculator, laundry detergent, or stash of Dr. Pepper.

I should have prepared for this. I should have bought the 24-pack of toilet paper on sale for $4.99. I should have socked away a spare toenail clipper. I should have known my duo would pack in laundry baskets and leave me wandering around the house with armloads of unfolded clothes.

"Is this the best we can do for towels?" their father asked as he used a bleach-bitten scrap from my arms.

I nodded toward the paper towels.

"Get used to it," I said. "Your sock drawer has been liquidated, too."

An eerie quiet swamps the house. That's because our son took one TV, and our daughter took the other, leaving us with a crotchety black-and-white with rabbit ears. It can't hold a channel, but makes a dandy flat surface for holding other stuff, such as laundry.

It's amazing what simple acts can trigger the pangs of plundered-nest syndrome. For example: having to substitute a pair of underwear for a missing shower cap, or having to thread an ugly orange extension cord through two rooms to substitute for the missing power strip.

As I replenish the nest with microwave-safe dishes, spare pillows, and such, I remind myself that time will ease the sting of plundered-nest syndrome.

I hope it happens before the little darlings pop back home for a visit and find something else—such as the coffee pot or this computer—to cart away.

Mom, It's Catherine

· *author unknown* ·

A teenaged girl had to stay at her girlfriend's overnight. She was unable to call her parents until the next morning.

"Mom, it's Catherine. I'm fine. My car broke down last night, and by the time I got to Julie's house it was well past midnight. I knew it was too late to call. Please don't be mad at me!"

By now, the woman at the other end of the phone realized the caller had the wrong number. "I'm sorry," she said, "I don't have a daughter named Catherine."

"Oh, Mom, come on! I didn't think you'd be *this* mad!"

If your parents never had children,
chances are you won't either.

—DICK CAVETT

It goes like this: The first child with a bloody nose is
rushed to the emergency room. The fifth child with a
bloody nose is told to go to the yard immediately
and stop bleeding on the carpet.

—ART LINKLETTER

You Rile the Kids Up,
You Put 'Em to Bed!

· joey o'connor ·

Who says guys don't know how to put the kids to bed? It's high time someone put this dastardly dad discrimination to rest. For years, guys have had to prove that they are both competent and capable at getting their kids to bed. I mean, how hard is it to get kids dressed, brushed, pottied, prayed, and tucked into bed?

Yes, every guy knows that his wife can zip through this necessary nightly ritual in less than ten minutes, but what's the big hurry? Guys know that their wives want to get the kids to bed early not because the kids need their rest, but because Mom needs hers—and besides, she wants to watch her favorite sitcom. Why make putting the kids to bed such a hurry-up-and-get-to-sleep system? Why make it so predictable? So routine? So one-dimensional? So boring?

Kids need to expand their horizons. They need their minds and bodies to be shaken and invigorated from that Jell-O induced state caused by too much TV and Sega. They need to push the limits. Break the envelope. Maybe even break (moms will love this) the sound barrier. Kids need to go to extremes, and that's why God made dads.

Let's take a vote: Ask your kids who they'd prefer putting them to bed, Mom or Dad? Hands down, Dad wins. Kids love it when Dad puts them to bed because that means they'll get to stay up *at least* forty-five minutes longer.

Start with "peeyamas." Once he gets the kids into their bedrooms, the first major challenge the dad faces is *finding* his kids' peeyamas. For all he knows, the peeyamas could be in a drawer, a closet, a Barney suitcase, a wastebasket, or a hamper, or (most likely) under the bed. How is he supposed to know where his kids put their peeyamas?

Once the peeyamas are located, the dad enters his first major battle of the evening when he squares off with his three-year-old daughter, who insists on choosing which pair of peeyamas she wants to wear.

"Honey, wear the Tinkerbell jammies."

"No, I wanna wear Winnie Pooh."

"Aw c'mon, just wear the Tinkerbell jammies. They look so cute on you."

"I hate Tinkerbell!"

"We don't say that word in this house. Winnie Pooh never says that word."

"Okay, but do I have to wear the Tinkerbells?"

Sad, pleading, puppy eyes.

"I guess not—you can wear the Winnie Poohs."

Even though her head doesn't fit through the opening for the right arm, the little DWARF (Daddy Wrapped Around Right Finger) insists she can put on the Winnie Pooh jammies just fine on her own. Winnie Pooh ends up backward and inside out, but she declares, "I meant to do that."

Knowing better than to mess with a willful woman, the dad sits back on his haunches and waits. Having already lost two battles, the dad now needs to compensate by launching a Tickle Monster counter-offensive. Seeing his daughter in her jammies makes it completely impossible not to tickle her. The dad was created for this purpose.

As she squeals in high-pitched laughter, his older son tears into the bedroom, wearing Photon Destroyer peeyamas and screaming, "DEATH TO THE ALIEN SLIME SUCKERS," whereby he proceeds to knee-drop dear old Dad to the floor. The dad plays dead and allows his kids to pound on him for 7.8 seconds. Like a phoenix rising from the ashes, the dad yells in a thundering voice, "BLANKET RAID!" His kids scream loud enough to break the neighbors' windows, and his wife, who happens to be watching her favorite sitcom downstairs, shakes her head and tells herself not to get up.

Quick as a flash, Dad grabs the covers off his daughter's bed and, in one fell swoop, covers both kids, who are now kicking and screaming like cats in a bag. Inevitably, both kids konk heads and Winnie Pooh begins crying.

"Okay," the Instigator asserts with a voice of authority and control, "settle down now."

Time to brush teeth.

Younger kids hate, oops, dislike using minty toothpaste because most dentist-recommended toothpaste feels hotter than Arizona asphalt in the middle of August. "It's too spicy," the kids cry as bubbly green foam drools down their faces.

Dads have a quick remedy for toothpaste burn victims. *Entertain them.* Putting a healthy dab on a toothbrush, the dad will work up a big glob of gooey foam and proceed to make toothpaste foam bubbles larger than his face. Not all dads aspire to such heights. Other variations on a theme include: Crazy Man Foaming at the Mouth, Foam on the Mirror, Foam Spit Tricks, and Foam Grenade.

Potty time.

During the potty portion of the bedtime routine, if Mom's in charge, the kids always have to go Number 1. If Dad's in charge, the kids always have to go Number 2.

Always.

From a physiological point of view, this is because twenty minutes of jumping on the bed, wrestling, and tickling produce enough activity to get the lower intestine moving and grooving.

From the psychological point of view, kids know that by sitting on the potty they can eke more time out of going to bed. By claiming to have to go Number 2, even giving the slightest mention of Number 2, they buy time because there's no way the dad is going to take any chances.

"You just sit there, honey, and take all the time you need. Want a book?"

Now for prayer time.

Prayer time is a major spiritual event in our home. One time when I was saying prayers with Ellie, our four-year-old, I felt a distinct little swipe across my forehead. I opened my eyes and looked at Ellie, who had a sneaky smile across her face.

"Ellie, what did you just do? Why'd you touch my forehead?"

"I wiped my goop."

That nostril deposit incited a furious tickling match and delayed prayer time another few minutes, which led to another series of distractions.

Distractions are what make it difficult for dads during prayer time. They're not used to fielding so many difficult questions. What is a dad really supposed to say when his kids ask how God turns the rain on or what Jonah looked like after he spent three days in the belly of a whale or why Noah allowed cockroaches and mosquitoes on the ark? Dads have a rough time answering such theological questions.

"Well, son, cockroaches play a very important role in making God laugh. You know how your mother and sisters jump up on the chairs and start screaming whenever they see an itty bitty cockroach? God thinks that's funny and that's why He created cockroaches. They're also the only ones who'll eat your mother's cooking, but that's just between us men."

By the time the fifth glass of water has been drunk and 473 monsters have been killed under the bed, in the closet, and outside the window, and the eleventh "Just one more question—" has been answered, it is an hour and forty-five minutes later, but the kids are exhausted and go right to sleep. The sitcom is long over and the dad's wife is fast asleep.

See, that wasn't so bad.

Piece of cake.

—Women Are Always Right and Men Are Never Wrong

With Friends Like These
· luci swindoll ·

One of the most delightful weekends I had spent since moving to California six months before was nearing an end. Two teenage girls approached me while I was counting out my vitamins. "What are all those pills for?" one of them asked. "Well," I explained, "these two are for beautiful eyes, this one is for long willowy legs, that little one is for pearly, white teeth..." and as I was waxing on, the other girl interrupted me with, "Haven't been taking them long, have you?"

—*Joy Breaks*

You Know There's a Baby in the House When . . .

· martha bolton ·

- The only dinner music they're playing is "Barney's Greatest Hits."
- A bib is part of your place setting.
- They're serving teething biscuits instead of dinner rolls.
- The host offers you your beverage in a Sit 'n Sip cup.
- All the eating utensils are rubber coated with Mickey Mouse handles.
- They're using Baby Wipes for napkins.
- The host offers to purée everyone's meat for them.
- The gravy has the distinct taste of formula.
- When the hostess offers you dessert, she spells it.
- The only accessories the hostess is wearing are a burp diaper on her left shoulder and a pacifier string around her neck.
- But you really know there's a baby in the house when the host and hostess start yawning at 7:30, and are face down in their mashed potatoes by 8 PM.

—Who Put the Pizza in the VCR?

The truth is that parents are not really interested in justice. They just want quiet!

—BILL COSBY

Human beings are the only creatures that allow their children to come back home.

—BILL COSBY

A Parent's Guide to Souvenir Shopping

· *marti attoun* ·

*E*very summer, parents navigate young travelers through the wonders of our fifty states—foot-tall plastic cups shaped like cowboy boots in Texas, tins of jackalope milk in New Mexico, placemats woven from kudzu in Alabama, and acres of giant pencils, cheap key chains, shot glasses, and back scratchers from sea to shining sea.

Oh, sure, the Grand Canyon is an impressive hole, but it's ho-hum beside the star attraction of any family vacation: souvenirs. As soon as young travelers exit their zip codes, they're eager to shop for memories of the trip.

With high gas prices, we can no longer afford shopper's remorse, so I offer my fellow travelers these souvenir-shopping tips learned the hard way—by making a U-turn in Tennessee after Elvis's voice-activated pelvis stopped swiveling twenty miles down the road, leaving a heartbroken ten-year-old who had blown her entire trip budget on the tacky treasure.

First, if the souvenir costs less than the batteries (never included) to activate it, be forewarned that it's engineered to last until you cross the state line. The talking outhouse bank that chatters a streak in Kansas every time the kids make a deposit will be as silent as the Sand Hills the minute you cross into Nebraska.

If the souvenir recipient has a creative name, such as Jingle or Apple, then don't waste your time flipping through racks of personalized mini license tags or plundering pegs of customized shoelaces. Stop twirling, and opt for the pocket mirror that says "sister" or "friend."

Saltwater taffy, although its rainbow colors practically shout "edible Americana," will yank out a loose baby tooth or knock an adult jaw out of alignment.

Surprises can be delightful, but stay away from the $2 grab bags in tourist traps. Where do you think they stash that over-the-hill saltwater taffy?

The brighter and gaudier the ink on the T-shirt, the cheaper it is and the more it will shrink. If it's as shocking yellow as highway lane paint and the ink stings your eyes and nose, you can probably snag the shirt for $5 or less. Buy XXL, even if the recipient is leaf-thin or a toddler.

Explain to young shoppers that the gift should match the recipient. I explained to my daughter that, yes, Grandma Mag would love the toothpick holder shaped like a West Virginia coal bucket, if only she had teeth. I seized this "teaching moment" to encourage brushing and flossing.

Likewise, the key chain shaped like the Minnesota state bird, a loon, is indeed a cool gift for an older cousin, except his pickup was just repossessed. Better to buy the $2.99 ink pen printed with the state map in case he is in a position to write a check someday. One more lesson about responsibility and budgeting.

Consider the dimensions of the souvenir if traveling in a compact car. Adults should know better, but I made the mistake of buying a gnarled shellacked driftwood coffee table from a kindly eighty-year-old folk artist in Wyoming. By the time I reached my Ozarks driveway, the table had traveled from folk art and funky to junky and chunky wedged between my knees and the cup holder. Furthermore, the passengers were equally weary of my souvenir and had begun hurling mean-spirited comments, such as, "Whatever possessed you to buy that ugly twisted stump anyway?" and "I've seen fancier sticks in that ditch by Granny's house."

Don't overlook the native freebies, such as globs of Spanish moss from the South, balsam-fir needles from the Adirondacks, and buckeyes from Ohio. These items are novelties and quite exotic on the home turf. Likewise, scrounge for catchy commercial freebies, such as matchbook covers featuring "Collinsville, Ill., The Horseradish Capital of the World" or "Alma, Ark., Spinach Capital of the World."

On the other hand, don't attempt to haul fresh or living native goodies, such as mullet from the Gulf of Mexico. They quickly decompose and the essence of vacation will linger longer than the credit card bills.

If you're approaching your home state and young travelers are frantic because they haven't bought anything yet for their best friends because you were too vacation-lagged to stop at the last fifteen tourist traps, don't get alarmed. Just take the nearest exit and head to the local discount store.

No one will know if you bought the coffee mug, bumper sticker, or plastic backscratcher in San Francisco or Dodge City, Kansas, when it says, "I (picture of heart) the U.S.A."

We (picture of heart) family vacations, too.

part two

Say Goodnight, Gracie!

Laughing Out Loud at Our Spouses

*Marriage is one of the few institutions that allow a
man to do as his wife pleases.*

—MILTON BERLE

Poor Ruth

· sheila walsh ·

Christian and I call her "Poor Ruth." The title confused her at first. She makes a good income as an interior designer, so it couldn't refer to her economic status. Her feet bother her a bit, but other than that, she's in good shape, physically. Christian explained our choice of title one day as she and Barry were heading out our front door to go shopping for rugs: "Miss Ruth, Mom and I call you 'Poor Ruth' because we know what it's like to go shopping with Dad. He's very . . . picky."

"A perfectionist," I added.

"Driven," Christian threw in.

"Obsessed even," I suggested.

Ruth smiled and said, "Oh, I've handled worse than your father," and with a naïve smile, she was gone.

We closed the door and looked at one another and said, "Poor Ruth."

When they returned several hours later, Christian and I were waiting at the front door. We escorted Ruth to the sofa. Christian helped her take off her shoes, and I put her legs up on a footstool. She looked at us with a glazed desperation.

"I know, Ruth," I said, "Don't try to talk!"

Five rugs—how hard could that be?

Barry has a gift for decorating, even if those who assist him require extensive therapy afterward. Our new home has travertine floors and hardwood, so we needed rugs to warm the rooms up. Poor Ruth told Barry that she had the perfect contact for nice rugs that wouldn't break the bank. When she staggered back into the house that day, I asked Barry if they had found what they were looking for.

He told me that the store was amazing, but he disagreed with the suggestion of the senior sales associate.

"I showed her pictures of the house and some of our furniture. She told me that we need deep navy and red rugs for our style of home, but I told her that we want black and red," he said.

"We do?" I said.

"We do," he replied with a confident smile.

Round One.

The first round of rugs arrived. There was one for the dining room, the living room, the den, my office, and a round rug for the entrance way. I thought they were lovely, but I was wrong! Barry said that they were too black and needed to have more red.

Round Two.

As I watched the men unfurl the rugs, I was sure these had to be right: more red and less black. Oh, foolish Galatian! Apparently the red was in the wrong place. You can have more red, but it can't be in just any old place.

Round Three.

As I opened the door to let the two men from the rug store in, we exchanged vocal glances: theirs said, *I beg you—like these!* Mine said, *If only it were that simple.*

I will spare you rounds four, five, six, and seven. By round eight, I had taken to hiding behind a tree in the backyard when the rugs arrived. On the evening of round eight, I asked Barry what the real issue was.

"The colors seem wrong," he said. "It's as if the black doesn't tone in with everything else."

"Do you remember that originally the rug lady suggested that dark blue might work better?" I asked.

"I still think that's wrong," he said as he pulled out a magazine on Italian design. "If you look at all the rugs in here they are . . . they are . . . actually they are . . . blue."

A Winning Round.

Round nine was a winner. As the rugs were carefully placed, Poor Ruth sat down on the sofa, and I am sure I could hear her quietly humming the "Hallelujah Chorus"! The blue rugs appear to be here to stay—there's even talk of cutting the tags off, but I'm not holding my breath just yet.

—*I'm Not Wonder Woman but God Made Me Wonderful*

Risky Business
· patsy clairmont ·

*M*y husband is a risk taker. Usually that has enhanced his life. Occasionally, though, his on-the-edge attitude gets him into a jam. And I'm not talking strawberry preserves.

One day Les was working on a project that required him to do some welding. In his desire to expedite things, he took a risk and didn't wear his safety glasses. He thought it might not matter since it wasn't an involved welding job. *Nyet.* It mattered. The tingling in Les's eyes began about ten o'clock that evening, but he decided to brave it out. The sandpaper feeling began about eleven. He thought he could endure it. The feeling of hot coals sizzling his eyeballs hit about midnight. He finally requested to be taken to the hospital or shot, whichever was fastest. I debated and then settled on the hospital.

We lived at a Boy Scout reservation in the country at the time. Our two young sons were asleep, and they both had school the following day. I decided to call in a friend to take Les to the clinic. I chose our dear friend and pastor, Marv. (Don't you know how thrilled he was to receive this honor.)

Les and Marv had been friends for years. They share a common interest in getting the other's goat. They are both playful, fun-loving fellows, who genuinely care for each other, although the casual observer might think there are moments when their jokes outweigh their caring.

Marv came immediately, extending concern and support. After arriving at the hospital and going through an eye check, Les learned there was no permanent damage. The doctor filled his eyes with cooling salve that immediately eliminated the pain. Then he taped

Les's eyes closed, covering them in bandages that wound around his head. Les looked like an escapee from King Tut's tomb. The doctor instructed him to leave the dressings on for eight hours.

Picture the opportunity this gave Marv—Les blindfolded and needing Marv to lead him around. Marv guided Les to the parking lot and then let him go, suggesting Les find the car. It was now 1 AM. There were only three cars in the lot. Les couldn't find any of them. (Remember Pin the Tail on the Donkey? Les's childhood training in this important game must have been inadequate. Car trunks and donkey rumps alike eluded him.) Marv finally ushered Les to the vehicle and brought him home.

At 2 AM, I heard laughter rolling in through my bedroom window. I was dozing, waiting to hear the outcome. I had expected the best, but I was not prepared for laughter.

I pulled back the shade and saw Marv holding onto Les's arm. Marv was telling Les how to avoid obstacles in his path.

I heard Marv say, "There's a step, Les; lift your foot."

Les lifted his foot in blind obedience. But there really wasn't a step, which left Les high-stepping it around the yard like a drum major.

Marv and Les were both guffawing, although Marv seemed to be laughing harder.

After I received the good news on Les's eyes, Marv headed home. We listened as he chuckled his way out to his car. Les and I laughed our way to bed.

The memory of that night could have been an eyesore for us all. But thanks to Marv, as we think back on it, we smile rather than wince. A little levity applied at the right moment can be a balm that lasts longer than the hurt, soothing a heavy heart. And yes, Les found a way to pay Marv back.

—*Normal Is Just a Setting on Your Dryer*

Think about this: No man was ever shot by
his wife while doing dishes!

—AUTHOR UNKNOWN

Try praising your wife even if it does frighten her at first.

—BILLY SUNDAY

The Rules

· joey o'connor ·

1. The FEMALE always makes the Rules.
2. The Rules are subject to change at any time without prior notification.
3. No MALE can possibly know all the Rules.
4. If the FEMALE suspects the MALE knows the Rules, she must immediately change some or all of the Rules.
5. The FEMALE is never wrong.
6. If the FEMALE is wrong, it's because of a flagrant misunderstanding that was a direct result of something the MALE did or said.
7. If Rule Six applies, the MALE must apologize immediately for causing the misunderstanding.
8. The FEMALE can change her mind at any time.
9. The MALE must never change his mind without the express written consent of the FEMALE.
10. The FEMALE has every right to be angry and upset at any time.
11. The MALE must remain calm at all times unless the FEMALE wants him to be angry and upset.
12. If the FEMALE has PMS, all Rules are null and void.

—*Women Are Always Right and Men Are Never Wrong*

A Dumpster So Divine

· marti attoun ·

I've been luxuriating in spending a full week with the world's largest trashcan parked in our driveway. I've never enjoyed a visitor more.

We rented the massive metal dumpster because we're ripping out carpeting and figured it'd be rude to throw it in the absentee owner's woods behind us. Besides, I was afraid that the billions of uprooted dust mites living in the carpet might have the homing instincts of salmon or rats and head directly back to our house.

Thus, we shelled out to rent a 22-foot-long blue metal bin, which I've quickly grown to cherish. You have no idea how handy it is to pull up beside it and park, step out of your car and casually fling your empty Starbucks cup into the air above its gaping maw.

With the investment in a week's worth of dumpster comes responsibility, though, to fill it to the brim and overflowing. After we'd dragged out all the carpet, pad, and trim wood, the dumpster was still only half full—or half empty—depending on your state of mind and whether your presidential candidate is up in the polls.

"We paid a fortune to rent this bin and, by golly, we're going to use it," my husband said as he stood in the middle of our garage and eye-balled its contents. He'd already pitched my bicycle-built-for-two into the dumpster and I'd had to climb in and tiptoe among strips of carpet nails to drag it back out. I've had the bike since the 1970s, it's wrapped in sentimental value, and I'm keeping it until one of us rusts.

"What about these louvered doors then?" he asked as he man-handled two saloon-style doors that we'd removed years ago from the dining room. "Are you emotionally connected to these ugly hunks of wood?"

Of course not. The louver memories belonged to the home's previous owners. We'd removed the doors to "open up" the room, but knowing that decorating whims change and the closed-up cave look could return tomorrow, we'd opted to keep them.

"This may be the best opportunity we ever get to dispose of these doors," my husband said. I could see the gleam in his eye as he could already imagine the liberating feeling that comes with tossing several pounds of stuff into the bin.

"Go for it," I told him.

Each passing day sent us scurrying through rooms, rounding up possessions to pitch. I thumbed my closet while chanting the "if-I-haven't-worn-it-in-twelve-years-I-never-will" rule and uncovered several shirts, jeans, and purses to feed to the bin. We dug into attic crawl spaces and dragged out parts of toys, a tacky pole lamp, and coffee tables that were just plain ugly.

"We could toss the kids' mattresses and box springs," my husband said. The oldest two moved their beds to their current abodes, but left behind their mattresses. They return home frequently for visits, though, and it seemed a bit unwelcoming to throw out their beds and make them sleep on the couch or floor.

Their father agreed, though it troubled him to see a foot of pricey space left at the top of the bin. "It just kills me that it's still a fourth empty," he said.

"But it's three-fourths full," I told him.

Are You Finished with That?

· sheila walsh ·

Do you experience times when there doesn't seem to be enough to go around? Bills are piling up faster than paychecks, and anxiety is creeping into your mind.

Many such moments have occurred to me, making me acutely aware that the bread on my plate came from the Lord because my cupboard was bare. When I was part of British Youth for Christ, I was paid a minimal salary. Usually I had just enough to keep me in hose and shampoo—and on my knees.

One of my memories from that time is of Phil, a staff evangelist, and his wife, who splurged one night and went to a nice restaurant for a steak dinner. While they were enjoying a lovely meal, Phil noticed that the man seated opposite them was leaving after only picking at his T-bone steak.

"More than three-quarters of that steak is left," Phil said to his wife indignantly. "What a waste!"

"Never mind what he's doing," she replied. "Enjoy your meal."

"But that's a huge piece of steak, and it'll go to waste," Phil continued. "They'll throw it out."

A few minutes passed, and then he said, "I'm sorry, but I just can't allow that to happen."

As he stood up, his wife hissed at him, "Sit down! What are you going to do?"

"Never you mind," he whispered. With that he sneaked over to the table, wrapped the large piece of meat in his napkin, and then slipped back into his seat.

"What did you do that for?" she asked in disbelief. "What are you going to do with it?"

"I'll give it to the dog," he said.

Two minutes later, the man who had been sitting at the table returned from the restroom to an empty plate. He called the waiter over and demanded to know what had happened to his meat. The poor waiter didn't have a clue as to its whereabouts, but he did casually wonder why that nice young couple was leaving without finishing their meal.

—Overjoyed!

Husband for Sale

· carol kent ·

*I*t happened again. Gene and I were in the car running errands, and I felt he was too close to the car in front of us. As the other automobile slowed down unexpectedly, I shrieked, "Watch Out!" Gene slammed on the brakes, and we were jolted forward.

As usual, he had plenty of room to stop, and we could have avoided this jerky reaction if I had kept my mouth shut. He was angry with me for being a back-seat driver—again. I told him I screamed because I honestly thought we were in danger and I believed my warning might save our lives. He was unconvinced. He pulled the car to the side of the road, looked in my direction, and said, "Do you want to drive?"

Now I was hurt. I wasn't trying to tell him how to drive. My scream had been involuntary. I did not plan to make him feel like an inadequate driver. Tears blocked my vision as I withdrew into my silent martyr role. (I feel so much more spiritual when I'm not speaking.) We drove home in the thick silence of anger, hurt, and misunderstanding.

As we mutely walked into the house, our conflict was still unresolved. I left Gene in the kitchen and walked into the next room. Opening my mail, I found this anonymous letter on my desk:

Dear Friend,

This letter was started by a woman like yourself in hopes of bringing relief to other tired and discontented women. Unlike most chain letters, this one does not cost anything.

Just bundle up your husband and send him to the woman whose name appears at the top of the list. Then add your name to the bottom of the list and send a copy of this letter to five of your friends who are equally tired and discontented. When your name comes to the top of the list, you will receive 3,325 men . . . and some of them are bound to be better than the one you gave up!

Do not break this chain! One woman did, and she received her own jerk back!

At this writing, a friend of mine had already received 184 men. They buried her yesterday, but it took four undertakers thirty-six hours to get the smile off her face.

We're counting on you,

—A Satisfied Woman

By the time I reached the middle of the letter, I was grinning. As I finished it, I was doubled up in uproarious laughter. My confused husband walked into the room wondering what had transformed his wounded wife. Looking up, my eyes met his. "I'm sorry," I said softly. "I overreacted."

"Me too," he responded, as he slipped an arm around my waist. His lips brushed the side of my face as he whispered in my ear, "Now, *what's so funny?*" His curiosity was killing him. And I couldn't keep a secret that was this hilarious.

"Listen to this," I said. I read the letter aloud, and both of us fell on the floor laughing until tears ran down our faces.

—*Detours, Tow Trucks, and Angels in Disguise*

Not Another One of Those Parties!

· joey o' connor ·

*I*f your wife likes clothes, beauty products, personal security devices, cookware, photo albums, long-distance communication, decorative stamp pads, vitamins, children's toys, and just about any product available on the face of this earth, chances are you married a party animal.

If your wife isn't a party animal yet, you're either recently married or recently lobotomized. In the latter case, I can't do anything to help you, except perhaps lend you my jigsaw for any corrective surgery you want to perform on yourself. In the former case, I have a warning: just you wait.

A recent discussion with my buddies confirms that all of our wives are party animals and that there is a racket going on in corporate America for housewives looking to earn a few extra dollars a week so they can "retire" in less than a year. It goes something like this—

Every few months or so, our wives get invited to attend "a party" hosted by a friend of a friend who is going to get a lot of "free" merchandise for hosting "the party." This enterprising hostess has invited everybody (a) whom she remotely knows, (b) who owes her a favor, and (c) who, like her, has no money.

Before I further extrapolate upon this unique cultural phenomenon, a brief explanation of previously mentioned terms is required. These all-female outings are not parties—they are department stores in motion. They are in-home sales meetings designed to sell you product, product, and, when you run out, more product.

Especially you soon-to-be-married or young married guys, did you get the gist of that last line? Read my lips: C-O-N-T-I-N-U-A-L-F-I-N-A-N-C-I-A-L-D-R-A-I-N!

Don't be hoodwinked. A party, as most people understand it, is a celebration for an important event such as a birthday, holiday, or special occasion like the Super Bowl. Buying or selling the latest gizmowhatchamacallit, cheese slicer, greaseless facial cream, toy puzzle, or chelated B vitamin does not justify calling these sales spiels "parties." To do so violates the traditional definition of the word. However, women will bend the traditional definition of this word to elevate the importance of the event and thus secure their exit from the house for the evening.

Next, the word *free* is very misleading. I do admit that I have allowed a certain number of these "parties" in our home. (Two. No more.) All on the premise that my wife would receive "free" merchandise based upon how much product was sold to everyone who couldn't afford it in the first place.

By the time my wife bought and mailed the party invitations, hired a professional house cleaner, and shopped for the party essentials of flowers, hors d'oeuvres, food, drinks, and dessert, we were in the hole to the tune of two hundred big ones.

For three weeks of addressing, mailing, shopping, cleaning, phoning, and getting me and the kids out of the house for the night, she received a "free" pizza dish valued at $35.

I'm still working at Taco Bell on the weekends to pay off that one.

Now, guys, don't be fooled. Your wife will say this is an important party she must attend. The person selling the product will have an important, corporate-sounding title like "Independent Sales Representative," "Personal Wardrobe Consultant," "Itchin' to Cook in da' Kitchen Connoisseur," "Global Dream Team Disco Machine," or "CEO of PO Box 591."

At the "party," your wife and the other poor women in attendance will learn dozens of personal enrichment exercises for slicing onions into perfect trapezoids, strategically placing pictures in photo albums, warding off would-be attackers with lemon-scented pepper spray, applying enough facial cream to grease a cement truck, and swallowing enough antioxidant vitamins to rid the entire Los Angeles basin of smog.

Even if your wife isn't especially interested in buying anything, like all the other women there, she will feel insufferably *sorry* for the priestess pitching the product at preposterous prices. Yes, your wife will feel *guilty* if she buys nothing. Not only will she feel guilty, she will also feel *embarrassed* if she walks out the front door empty-handed. And why not?

The hostess is counting on her. Her "free" booty is based upon total sales.

The sales lady is counting on her. Her entire financial future is at stake.

Your wife's friends are counting on her. There is strength in numbers, and when each wife tells her husband that "everybody" was buying, your wife can't stand the idea of being the lone fasting shark in this financial feeding frenzy.

And so, your wife will give in to guilt and put you in the poorhouse.

All my buddies and I agree that, if our wives could have demonstrated a little financial control at these parties, by now we could have paid in cash for the trips to Europe, cruises in the Bahamas, and the lazy days on the sun-soaked beaches of Hawaii they all dream about. Can we help it if they've traded sparkling diamonds for laundry soap and deodorant?

If there is ever a fire in his house, my buddy Scott says the first thing he's grabbing is his wife's creatively designed photo album. He's got more money invested in that thing than anything else in the house. The only reason my other buddy Glen keeps his wife's vitamin business going is so he can file a Schedule C loss on their tax return. To top it off, my other buddy Brad is determined to print his own catalog to unload the thousand dollars of inventory his wife purchased to start her own decorative stamping business.

Sorry, Brad. We ain't buying.

With all this haranguing about in-home sales meetings, you must think I'm a real party pooper. I'm not. Honest. If your wife is going to a lingerie party, give her the checkbook and VISA card, take a second on the house, borrow from your kid's college savings—anything. With this important purchase, you can both throw your own little get-together and really become party animals.

I e-mailed these comments to some of my closest pals. We do have a united campaign against our wives' party fever. Cracking the lid on this party circuit is a dangerous job. I would like to thank Robert "Bob" Clippinger for his security-conscious contribution.

The e-mail reads:

Joey,

Got your comments and was busy laughing until I got wind of the contract on your life by MOPS (Mothers of Preschoolers) International. The next time you send this out, you ought to use a pen name or else hire a bodyguard. You just broke the secret domain of female parties, and don't think for a moment that they will let you out alive. As a matter of fact, unless you stop distributing this radical material, I will no longer be able to associate with you . . . I have a family!!!

See you???
Bob

—*Women Are Always Right and Men Are Never Wrong*

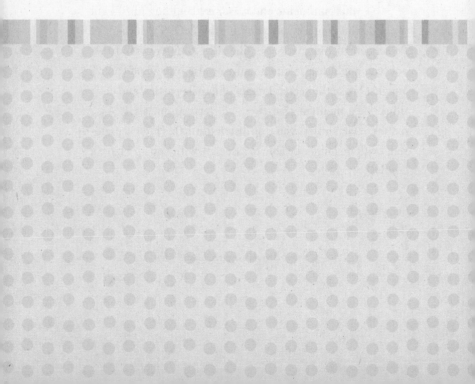

Women like silent men. They think they're listening.

—AUTHOR UNKNOWN

Yawn: *n.* Nature's way of letting married
men open their mouths.

—AUTHOR UNKNOWN

After fifty-four years of marriage, Billy Graham was asked
his secret to long-term love and successful marriage.
His reply?
"Ruth and I are happily incompatible!"

You've Got Male

· anita renfroe ·

I am married to a man who is the definitive "offensive driver," and I don't mean that in the sense that he is offending people; he just thinks every run to the grocery store is like fourth and goal and that he must power through to the end zone.

In the past five years, he's gotten worse—or I've gotten more aware. Maybe both. Perhaps when I was younger, I was too busy replacing pacifiers in kids' mouths or unwrapping their Happy Meal toys to pay adequate attention. Whatever the case, his driving is a source of blood pressure elevation and adrenaline surge for me.

John actually believes he has some sort of superpowers. All men believe this about some area of their life. You might think your man is an exception, but I guarantee that you are just not paying close enough attention. John's area of superpower delusion is in the imaginary force field that he believes moves in front of our vehicle, something akin to a Cosmic Cow Pusher. For those of you not rural enough to know what a cow pusher is, it's that V-shaped thing that sticks out front of old-timey trains. This would push cows off the tracks so they wouldn't mess up the train wheels (gross). Anyway, John believes that by the mere force of his will he can continue accelerating (even though the car ahead has large red brake lights lighting up) and will be able to move this obstruction from his path with his Cosmic Cow Pusher. He also suffers from this delusion with regard to traffic lights; he believes that by continuing to accelerate, he can somehow force the light to change.

He does this to pedestrians as well. At the Kroger parking lot, they have that stripy section painted in the middle—the one that means, "This is where the people preoccupied with their groceries, carts, cell phones, and car keys are walking. Stop and let them be distracted without killing our customers, please." My husband likes to pull up to the edge of the stripes and keep rolling into the stripe area while motioning for the people to walk on across. This is very confusing for them, because they don't know if he is going to stop, or just keep rolling and hit them. So they do the little "indecisi-jig"— you know, that little two-step dance you do when you don't know whether to step out or step back. John sees absolutely nothing wrong with keeping them guessing. So I just slink down in the truck seat and hope nobody recognizes us.

I did experience a moment of revelation one night when we were driving to Florida. It explained so much. John kept saying, "Did you see that deer? They're all over tonight." I never saw any of them. After the tenth time he said this, I responded, "How are you seeing all of them and I am seeing none of them?" He actually said, "I'm watching the ditches." Suddenly, I felt a wave of revelation sweep over me: *That explains everything. All this time I was under the impression that it was the driver's job to watch the road, but apparently, if you are male, you watch the ditch.* He always points out to me that he hasn't killed us yet. Somehow this does not comfort me.

—*Purse-Driven Life*

The one thing that unites all human beings, regardless of age, gender, religion, economic status, or ethnic background, is that, deep down inside, we *all* believe that we are above-average drivers.

—DAVE BARRY

Marriage has no guarantees. If that's what you're looking for, go live with a car battery.

—ERMA BOMBECK

I got gaps. You got gaps. We fill each other's gaps.

—ROCKY

Messages

· patsy clairmont ·

When our big twenty-fifth anniversary arrived, Les bought me nothing. Of course, that's what I had asked for, but what does that have to do with anything? Mates are supposed to be able to decipher mixed messages. Les is supposed to discern when I mean "absolutely no" from when I mean "sort of no."

Here's the thing. Wives don't want to shoulder the responsibility of giving husbands permission to be extravagant. It frees us from guilt if we say no and our husbands don't listen to us, which of course is what we're hoping will happen. That way we can say to others, "I told him not to do this, but he did it anyway."

Les and I agreed to take a trip south as a shared gift, but I was hoping for something a little more personal. I must have been too convincing when I said, "If you get me anything I'll be mad." Maybe I should have said, "If you get me anything I might, in a minute way, be temporarily displeased."

Most of us gals secretly hope for a good "show and tell" kind of gift, especially for our twenty-fifth. It's difficult to flaunt—I mean show—a trip to your friends.

I decided to subtly retract my giftless declaration at the first appropriate moment.

A week later Les dropped me off for a speaking engagement and announced he was going to the area mall for his morning coffee. The word "mall" flashed like a neon opportunity.

With more zeal and clarity than I meant to display, I blurted out, "Why don't you buy me something!"

Oops, I probably confused him by being that . . . that . . . honest. Not that I'm not always honest . . . sort of.

When Les came back to pick me up, he had heard the message, for there, on the front seat, was a beautifully wrapped gift. I admired it for a moment and then began to remove the floral paper. Inside were layers of soft white tissue secured with a gold seal that read "lingerie."

Well, this was proof that honesty did pay; I was getting what I deserved. So what if it was a week late.

I gently pulled back the last layer of tissue and lifted out my ... my ... prehistoric gift. What unfolded was a long white cotton nightshirt sporting a gregarious dinosaur wearing a lopsided hat.

—*God Uses Cracked Pots*

You Should Know How I Feel

· joey o' connor ·

*L*et's face one important fact about men and women: It is impossible for women to know what men are thinking, and it is equally impossible for men to know what women are feeling. The chasm between understanding a man's world and a woman's world is so huge that universities are actually being formed to help married couples better understand one another.

In my research to better understand the psycho-social-mental-chemical-temperamental differences between men and women, I came across The Whatsamatta Online University at http://www.menarealwayswrong.com. Adhering to the rigorous academic standard of giving proper credit where credit is due, I found no source for the following information. Therefore, the author of this piece is recognized as anonymous. On second thought, he probably meant to do that. The university is offering the following courses for guys to better understand why the female mind gets so frustrated with men. Here are their top ten suggested classes:

1. The Remote Control—Overcoming Your Dependency
2. Romanticism—Other Ideas Beyond Sex
3. How Not to Act Younger Than Your Children
4. You Cannot Always Wear Whatever You Please
5. We Do Not Want Sleazy Underwear for Christmas (Just Give Us Credit Cards)
6. The Weekend and Sports Are Not Synonymous
7. You, the Weaker Sex
8. Parenting Roles Beyond Initial Conception
9. Get a Life—Learn to Cook

10. You Don't Look Like Mel Gibson, Especially When Naked

For women who wish to probe for signs of intelligent life in the minds of men, there was also another web site offered by The Whatsamatta Online University at http://www.cantlivewiththem-cantlivewithoutem.com. The university recommends the following ten courses for women:

1. Get a Life—Learn to Kill Spiders Yourself
2. You Can Change the Oil Too
3. Romanticism—The Whole Point of Caviar, Candles, and Conversation
4. Attainable Goal—Catching a Ball Before It Stops Moving
5. We Do Not Want Ties for Christmas (Just Wear the Sexy Lingerie I Gave You)
6. Payday and Shopping Are Not Synonymous
7. How to Do All Your Laundry in One Load and Have More Time to Watch Football
8. Why It Is Unacceptable to Talk about Feminine Hygiene in Mixed Company
9. It's Okay to Do It Outside of the Bedroom
10. How Not to Sob Like a Sponge When Your Husband Is Right

Have you ever thought of becoming a brain surgeon in order to better understand your spouse? Wouldn't it be a whole lot easier if your spouse thought and felt just like you? Wouldn't it be nice to avoid going to extremes simply by plugging your brain into your spouse's brain and downloading all the information you need to understand what they're thinking or feeling? If you're frustrated at your husband's lack of sensitivity for your feelings or if you're upset at your wife's attempt at brain surgery to figure out what you're thinking, remember that your spouse is not wired to think or feel like you.

Though men and women share similar qualities and character-istics, women do have a predisposition to be more intuitive and feel-oriented than men. On the other lobe, men have the predisposition to be more reason- and logic-oriented than women. These predisposi-tions, along with how men and women are socialized in our society, explain why men are the way they are and why women are the way they are. So, trying to change your husband or wife so they will better understand your wants and needs is next to impossible. What you can do, though, is first understand your spouse's wiring so you can better communicate what you want and need from them.

I hope this valuable information will help you and your spouse learn once and for all that it's all about the electronics!

—*Women Are Always Right and Men Are Never Wrong*

Up and Adam

· todd and jedd hafer ·

dam is one of our favorite Bible characters for several reasons. He was always a shoo-in for Who's Who. He never had a mother-in-law. He didn't have to worry about other guys trying to steal his girl. The toilet seat being up was never an issue. And he never had to hear those fateful words, "Why can't you be more like _____?"

But most of all, we like Adam because he was—and this isn't widely known—the world's first comedian. In fact he invented the joke. One day, Eve asked him, "Adam, do you love me?"

He shrugged his bare shoulders and said, "Who else?"

We'd like to introduce you to Adam, the world's pioneer humorist, as he goes about his daily activities in Eden. Look, there he is sneaking up behind Eve and putting his hands over her eyes.

"Guess who-oooooo?"

"Oh, Adam, you are so silly!"

"Ah, you guessed right again! You're pretty smart for someone made from a rib!"

"Let's not go there, dust-boy!"

"Touché, Eve. Hey, I've been meaning to ask you something. If we decide to have kids and one of them is a boy, can we name him Abel?"

"Abel? What kind of name is that? It's rather sheepish. And then I suppose we'll have to name his siblings Ready and Willing? Nuh-uh—especially not if they're girls. I kind of prefer Cain as a boy's name."

"Cain? Oh, spare me. That rhymes with pain. A boy named Cain is gonna be nothing but trouble, Eve."

"Let's just not discuss it right now, Adam. Let's talk about something else. Like what you are wearing."

"But I'm wearing nothing."

"Precisely. And nothing is so, so . . . last season. I'm bored with both our wardrobes."

"So you're complaining that you have nothing to wear?"

"Precisely. Maybe we should try putting on some fig leaves for a change."

"Eve are you kidding? Wear those itchy, scratchy fig leaves on our bodies? I'll tell you something: I wouldn't be caught dead walking out of this garden wearing fig leaves!"

"Whatever you say, Adam. You know, all this arguing is making me hungry. Let's go down by the peach tree and have some dinner."

"That's a great idea, honey. You know how I love peaches. You are so thoughtful! There's just no other woman in the world for me."

"You can say that again, Adam."

"And after dinner, we can go for a walk into the center of the garden."

"I don't know, Adam. That serpent likes to hang out down there. He creeps me out."

"Ah, Eve, relax. What harm can a little snake do?"

—*Snickers from the Front Pew*

A mother, much against her better judgment, finally gave in and bought the children a dog with the understanding that they would care for it. They named the dog Laddy. It wasn't long before the responsibility fell to the mother, and she found that she was taking care of the dog all by herself. Since the children did not live up to their promise, she decided to sell Laddy.

When the children returned from school, she gave them the news.

One of them sorrowfully said, "We'll miss him."

Another said, "If he wouldn't eat so much and wouldn't be so messy, could we please keep him?"

But Mom stood her ground. "No. I'm sorry, children. It's time to take Laddy to his new home."

"Laddy?" the children gasped. "We thought you said Daddy."

part three

Dogs, Cats, and Caribou!

Laughing Out Loud at Our Animal Friends

I am fond of pigs. Dogs look up to us. Cats look down on us.
Pigs treat us as equals.

—WINSTON CHURCHILL

Help, Lord, There's a Cat on My Face

· sheila walsh ·

With all my years of traveling, I've slept in some strange places. My great comfort when I'm far away from home is that the Lord never sleeps but watches over me whether I'm in Bangkok, Britain, or Boise, Idaho.

Some of the most powerful memories are from my time as a youth evangelist in Europe. In Britain, an evangelist or singer would never stay in a hotel after an evening meeting. Hospitality—and I use that word advisedly—would be extended from a member of the local church. That hospitality is what drove me to lift my eyes to my sleepless God to extend his help.

I remember staying with an old lady in Bristol, England, who had forty-three cats. I like cats, but forty-three are about forty-two cats too many for me. I drank my cup of cocoa with cat fur in it and then thanked my hostess and headed to bed.

"My little darlings will follow you!" she sang out after me.

I turned to see a plague of fur flow after me. "That's all right," I said. "I can find my room."

"It's where my darlings sleep, too!" She smiled as she delivered this good news.

Fluffy, Muffy, and the gang made themselves comfortable on the bed, in my suitcase, and in my toilet bag. We were a family.

As I went to sleep, I prayed, "Lord, please keep these beasts off me while I'm sleeping."

I woke up to find I was suffocating. I must be in a cave, a tunnel, I was drowning . . . no, it was worse than that. "Help, Lord, there's a cat on my face!"

Is it ever hard for you to close your eyes at night? Do you worry about what tomorrow will hold or if you will be safe until morning? Psalm 121 makes it clear that God never closes his eyes. He is always watching over you . . . even if you have cat fur in your mouth.

—Overjoyed!

A stranger noticed a sign reading: DANGER! BEWARE OF DOG! posted on the glass door of a little country store. Inside, he noticed a harmless old hound dog asleep on the floor beside the counter. He asked the store manager, "Is that the dog folks are supposed to beware of?"

"Yup, sure is," he replied.

The stranger couldn't help but smile in amusement. "That certainly doesn't appear to be a dangerous dog to me. Why did you post that sign?"

"Well," the owner replied, "before I posted that sign, people kept tripping over him."

Princess Fur-Face

· marilyn meberg ·

Whata'ya say we change the furniture around?" Ken queried one Saturday morning as we were finishing our last cups of coffee/tea. "Let's put the couch by the window and the two chairs facing the fireplace." I had learned years before to trust Ken's fine eye for furniture placement.

"Sounds good to me, Babe," I said, "but do you have the stamina for Ashley's neurotic response?"

Ashley was our cocker spaniel who reacted strongly against all visual changes. She wanted things to remain in their accustomed spots. If they didn't, she had one of her "spells." It didn't matter how big or small the change; each warranted a protest. Let me give you an example.

A friend popped in on me one morning and for some reason just dropped her purse in the middle of the floor as we made our way to the "chat chairs" by the window. (This was before the rearrangement.) Several moments later Ashley, who hated to miss anything, came trotting into the room. Spotting my friend's purse in the middle of the floor, she skidded to a stiff-legged halt, stared briefly at the purse, and went into a dramatic fit of barking. Slowly circling the purse, she barked, growled, and scowled until my friend finally placed her purse behind the chair. Gradually Ashley settled down, but it was obvious the visit was ruined for her.

As Ken pondered the price to be paid for furniture rearrangement, he noted that Ashley was out on the deck dozing in the sun. She might not notice what was going on until the dastardly deed was done.

Several hours later Ashley roused herself from her siesta and ambled into the house. She immediately assessed that unauthorized changes had occurred in her absence. After barking herself nearly hoarse, she flounced out of the living room and stayed in her "deep area" for several days. We delivered her food and water. Gradually she came to realize that the couch was now in a far better spot for her because she was able to see out the window. (Of course she was allowed on the furniture!) This made it possible for her to visually patrol the neighborhood without leaving the comforts of home.

Perhaps the greatest trauma Princess Fur-Face had to endure was when we got a new car. Ashley's sleep area was in a small room adjoining the garage, and although the car wasn't fully visible to her, it was in close proximity.

On the first night of their cohabitation, Ashley, who had not yet been introduced to the new car, scampered down the stairs to bed as was her custom. We stood behind the closed door holding our breath. No sound . . . no barking . . . no response at all. Ken's theory was that because it was dark, Ashley couldn't see the car. Our intention was to later, in the daylight, gradually coax her into an accepting relationship with the new vehicle.

Around 1 AM we were awakened by the sound of frantic, ferocious barking. Ashley had discovered the car. Fearing she'd disturb the neighbors, Ken flew down the stairs, scooped up Ashley along with her bed, and deposited her in our room, something Ken normally refused to do. She grumbled and complained the rest of the night, but at least she didn't bark.

Because Ken drove the car to work during the day, I had no opportunity to ease Ashley into a spirit of charitableness about the car. Each night she seemed to forget about the alien in the garage when she first went to bed, then rediscover it sometime after midnight.

At 2 AM on the fourth night of Ashley's histrionics, Ken exasperatedly dragged himself out of bed and announced he had just come up with a plan that required that we both get dressed and take Ashley for a ride.

"Are you going to dump her out of the car somewhere in another county?" I asked cautiously as I threw on jeans and a sweatshirt.

"Trust me," was all he said.

Ken thrust a squirming, growling, barking cocker into my arms, and we got in the monster car to begin what Ken said would be the "taming ride." For at least an hour Ashley was a bundle of growling rigidity in my arms. With the radio playing soft music and both of us stroking Ashley with words of love and encouragement (none of which we felt at that moment), Ashley began to relax. An hour and a half later and miles from home, she went limp in my arms and fell asleep. From that moment on, Ashley had peace about her metal roommate. In fact, one of her favorite activities became riding in that car.

I hate to tell you how closely I identify with Ashley at times. There are God-gifts I have fought so fervently only to find that once I yield my resisting spirit I reap incredible benefits. For example, I certainly don't overly resist the concept of grace, but I've tried to earn it a million times. I seem to tenaciously cling to the mistaken notion that I've got to be good enough in order to deserve grace. How many times does God have to hold my rigidly resisting spirit until finally, with celestial music in my ears, I relax and embrace his gift?

Ashley learned with just one ride.

—*Extravagant Joy*

Researchers have discovered that dogs can comprehend a vocabulary of 2,000 words, whereas cats can only comprehend 25–50 words. No one ever asks how many words the researchers can comprehend.

—AUTHOR UNKNOWN

Did you ever walk into a room and forget why you walked in? I think that's how dogs spend their lives.

—SUE MURPHY

In the Company of Critters
· karen scalf linamen ·

Kacie loves critters.

In fact she loves animals of all kinds, including invisible ones.

Case in point: she's got this imaginary friend named Tito.

She began talking about Tito a couple years ago. Best we can tell, Tito is a dog. He also has a girlfriend named Marie.

Sometimes Tito has a bit of a mean streak. Like the time I was driving and looked into my rearview mirror and saw Kacie sitting quietly in her car seat, tears streaming down her face.

"Kacie! What's wrong?"

She blinked. "Tito bit me."

All our friends at church know about Tito. One man in particular enjoys teasing Kacie about Tito. Practically every time he sees Kacie, Herschel asks, "How's Tito?"

Sometimes Kacie tells him. Increasingly, however, Kacie merely crosses her arms and purses her lips as if to say, "Oh puhlease, not again."

One day another friend overheard Herschel teasing Kacie. His curiosity piqued, Condall just had to ask, "Who in the world is Tito?"

Herschel told him.

Condall thought the whole thing was great and figured he'd get in on the fun. Squatting eye-level with Kacie, he grinned and said, "Hey Kacie, how's Tito?"

Kacie never even blinked. She eyeballed him back and said levelly, "Tito's dead."

So Herschel and Condall killed Tito. Tito stayed dead for several months until Marie managed to bring him back to life. Kacie explained that Marie did this with some sort of magic stones. I figured Kacie and Marie assumed this was safe to do because Herschel and Condall had finally stopped asking about Tito.

Tito may have a mean streak, but he seems to appreciate his privacy.

When Kacie's not playing with invisible friends, the other critters she loves are garden critters. She's always begging me to help her find pill bugs, June bugs, crickets, even snakes.

She really loves snakes. Little baby garden snakes. She gets this death grip around their little bodies and hangs on tight.

I always watch her closely when she's playing with snakes. I'm not worried about her physical safety as much as her psychological health. I don't think it's healthy for a child to have to live with the fact that she inadvertently squeezed the life out of a baby snake with her bare hands.

Besides, Kacie's probably already going to need therapy, what with having to kill Tito off like that.

In any case, the other day Kacie and I were wrapping up a day spent in the garden. Kacie had just spent the afternoon with many of her favorite critters. She had collected roly-pollies, chased crickets, prodded worms, studied ants, and befriended several moths.

It had been a well-populated afternoon, although if I remember right, Tito was nowhere to be seen (which, come to think of it, is probably to be expected for an invisible dog).

On our way inside for dinner, Kacie needled me with several dozen questions about worms and crickets and pill bugs and ants. I found myself explaining how all these critters and many others form a sort of community. I told her that the worms aerate the soil and the bees pollinate the flowers and the crickets . . . well, I don't really know what crickets do, but I'm sure I made something up and managed to sound fairly credible in the process.

I told her that each critter was important, and that our garden just wouldn't be the same without them all.

And I've been thinking about that conversation ever since.

I'm part of a community too. I won't say if I'm more like the hardworking ant or the social butterfly (nectar, anyone?), but my point is that I am part of a community of critters, and every one of us has a unique role to fill. There are the quiet laborers, the encouragers, the movers and the shakers, the problem solvers, and the huggers. In my community (as in yours, no doubt) there are even a few well-meaning pests.

What a privilege it is to have these folks in my life.

You know, the Bible encourages us not to forsake fellowship with other believers. I think it's because we really do need each other. Not a one of us can thrive isolated and on our own.

Not even Tito.

He might be a little shy around Herschel and Condall, but I hear he's sticking close to Kacie and Marie these days.

They knew right where to find those magic stones, after all.

—*Welcome to the Funny Farm*

Nothing in the world is friendlier than a wet dog.

—AUTHOR UNKNOWN

Outside of a dog, a book is probably man's best friend;
inside of a dog, it's too dark to read.

—GROUCHO MARX

Developing 'Sponsibility
· marilyn meberg ·

Our daughter, Beth, came tearing into the house one morning with a look on her seven-year-old face that meant *I have an idea too big for the universe!*

"Mama," she began, "we could have a horse! It could play in the backyard, drink from the swimming pool, and sleep in the garage. We have plenty of room. I just decided!" Whenever Beth "just decided" anything, it took a good bit of energy as well as creativity to move her away from her conviction.

She countered each of my arguments against a horse with the same statement, "My teacher says taking care of a pet helps ya learn 'sponsibility." Every now and then Beth would broaden her argument with, "I need to get that 'sponsibility sometime, ya know."

Ultimately, we worked our way down from a horse to a hamster. She reluctantly agreed one could learn 'sponsibility with a small animal just as well as with a large one. That issue settled, Beth and I went to the pet store, where she selected Sugar from a squirming throng of other hamsters. We also bought a Plexiglas cage, an exercise wheel, and special hamster food guaranteed to maintain Sugar's robust health.

Initially, the whole family took an active interest in Sugar, but her utter indifference to us squelched any anticipation we may have had of meaningful relatedness. After all, the whole purpose was to give Beth an opportunity to develop 'sponsibility.

Several weeks after Sugar became a family member, Beth announced she was sure Sugar was bored. We all felt slightly bruised. How could she be bored? She had a lovely cage, wheel, food, and all of us at her disposal should she want us.

Beth described a Plexiglas round ball that her friend Suzie had for her hamster. She put the hamster in the ball, snapped it shut, and the hamster simply roamed around the house in this little ball. When the hamster moved, the ball moved.

So, in an effort to relieve the tedium in Sugar's life, Beth and I once again headed for the pet store and purchased a roaming ball. I don't know who was more delighted with that ball, Sugar or me. We would put her in the ball, click it shut, and off she would go in a flash, bumping into furniture and walls, righting herself, and then speeding off in another direction. It was rather like watching a miniature bumper car on the loose.

What particularly gave me a giggle was guests' reactions as Sugar would flash through a room. A first-time visitor who caught a glimpse of this self-propelled, fur-filled ball moving rapidly and haphazardly through the house and then quickly disappearing found the experience a bit unsettling. Ken and I often pretended we hadn't seen it and professed puzzlement as visitors tried to describe their sightings.

As Sugar's enthusiasm for her ball began to wane, we were all concerned she might be slipping back into her former state of boredom. Often we would find her in her ball dozing behind a couch, or under a table. She made little effort to explore anymore. We know, of course, that hamsters are nocturnal creatures and do most of their wild living at night, but, nonetheless, Sugar was exhibiting signs of lassitude. What could we do?

Beth suggested we buy Sugar a "sky restaurant." Suzie had purchased one for her hamster, and it had seemed to raise its flagging spirits considerably. We agreed that might be the answer for Sugar. Later, as I watched her zip up the little cylindrical tube that led to a separate floor, I wondered what would happen to her fragile psyche when she discovered that despite its name, food was never served up there in the sky restaurant's tower.

Predictably, the sky restaurant soon lost its appeal. That made perfect sense to me—the promise of food that never appeared would certainly put me in a slump. With some concern, we realized Sugar occasionally whiled away her time by gnawing on the far-right corner of her cage. It occurred to all of us she might be working on an escape route, but surely she couldn't gnaw through Plexiglas. Surely the best she could manage would be a dime-size opening.

One night around 2 AM, I awakened to an odd noise. I poked Ken into startled awareness, and of course, he heard nothing. I lay there as he immediately fell back to sleep and ultimately decided he was right. It was nothing.

Then it sounded again. A hurrying, scurrying sound seemed to come from under the bed. It then trailed quickly to the dressing area and into the adjoining bathroom. I leaped out of bed, grabbed the flashlight, and beamed it into the bathroom. Sugar was staring back at me with her little cheeks and neck stuffed so full of something she was barely recognizable in her lumpiness. Carefully setting her and her cargo back in the cage (the top was off; how had that happened?), I watched with delight as Sugar proceeded to spew forth from her mouth one brightly colored wooden bead after another. The beads would hit the Plexiglas wall and then roll into silence. One, two, three, four, five, six . . . finally, seventeen beads later, little Sugar had disgorged her treasures.

Apparently in her early-morning foray throughout the house, Sugar had discovered the beads under Beth's bed. (Beth and Suzie had been making necklaces to complement their second-grade wardrobes.) I scooped up the beads, thanked Sugar for a wonderful giggle, and went back to bed.

A few weeks later, I returned from work to discover Sugar had escaped again. She had gnawed through the cage corner and was nowhere to be seen. The slider screen to the backyard was slightly ajar, so I assumed she had ventured outside. But my searching was unsuccessful. This time she was gone for good.

When I told Beth about Sugar's escape, instead of the pained response I had anticipated, Beth was relieved. Her philosophical response was, "That's probably best, Mama. Nothing seemed to make her happy anyway." Noticing my lingering concern, Beth added, "Try not to take it too hard. You did everything you could." Several hours later, she followed me into my study and said, "Would a horse make you feel better?"

—*I'd Rather Be Laughing*

Don't Make Eye Contact

· patsy clairmont ·

*B*ecause fear ruled my life for years, I never expected I would one day have the thrill of traveling to other parts of the world, first to Israel and then Africa. Me—Israel? Africa? Wow! Even now, as I write this, I'm flabbergasted.

Our trip to Africa took nine flights and eleven days to make memories that will last a lifetime.

Going so far to such a different land presented me with a number of mental obstacles I had to scale. First were the shots. I'm not afraid of needles, but because I tend to be drug sensitive, I can work myself into a dither anticipating a reaction. So I can't tell you what relief I felt to go with my Women of Faith pals to have the injections. There really is something about numbers that helps, especially when those people are full of faith and fun.

Once the shots were in order, the next discomfort for me was flying over the ocean, which turned out to be a nonissue once we were off the ground. I wondered if all that water beneath us would bother me, but it didn't. That fear was quickly put to rest; of course, it helped that we had a smooth ride.

We had been warned not to drink the water or even brush our teeth with tap water while in Africa. We also were cautioned about our food choices, where we ate, and not to leave our hotel unaccompanied while in Nairobi. The list was detailed and could have become mental fodder for an ex-phobic. In fact, I could have worked myself into a dither if I hadn't maintained good thought boundaries. Add to that, when we arrived, I noted armed guards outside the hotel and for a moment wondered if FedEx could overnight me back to Michigan.

A few days later we flew out of Nairobi in a single-engine plane over the savannahs to the Masai Mara Lodge. Our bush pilot was young, which gave me pause. Actually any pilot on such a runt of a plane would have deepened my prayer life. I just wasn't sure I wanted to fly in such a tiny aircraft with only one engine. But again I was surprised that once I was onboard I enjoyed the flight. Even landing on a dirt path in the middle of nowhere was exciting.

Just so you get the picture of the petite aircraft we flew in, let me say our luggage had to be driven to the lodge because the airplane couldn't safely carry that much weight. Hello. After we were weighed, we were assigned seats to balance the aircraft according to the number that had rudely popped up.

I was praying nobody sneezed or even turned around lest we head for the earth prematurely. Actually, it turned out the only one who couldn't sit still during the flight was neck-craning me, because I was trying not to miss the spectacular landscape out the windows.

After arriving at the Masai Mara Lodge, we journeyed to a remote village where we were to visit a family that lived in the hills in a hut. I was looking forward to it even though the ride was hard and jostling.

The visit was touching, but part of the adventure of that day still lay before us—we just didn't know it. The ride back to our lodge, which should have taken three hours, took five. We were tossed and bounced every which way but out the window (only because it was closed).

Unbeknownst to us, while we had been village visiting, hard rains had fallen for miles around our lodge and had left the cratered roads in fragile condition. We were still miles from the lodge's safety, evening was falling, and we were seeing all kinds of wild, I repeat, wild animals on the savannah. Then we spotted an armed government official on the road ahead. As we neared, he flagged us down to chat with our driver. The driver was told he couldn't proceed on the roads, but we must instead travel on the water-soaked savannah.

As bad as the roads were, may I just say the savannah was much worse. To keep from sinking axle-deep, the driver had to floor it. We all hung on as we careened up and down water-filled ruts and ditches. At one point I spotted, through the sprays of water off our tires, a hippo just a few feet away. My stress level rose, but to my surprise I was enjoying the raucous ride.

Then it happened. Just ahead of us was a herd of water buffalo. Now, if you haven't been up close and personal with a water buffalo, they are about the size of a motor home pulling a U-Haul. Their horns start on their heads, swirl halfway down around their faces, and then curl back up at the ends. Sort of like a flip hairdo. (Think Doris Day in the fifties. Only Doris was cute.)

Water buffalo give new meaning to the phrase "whipped with an ugly stick," and their dispositions match. Here is my suggestion: If you travel to Africa and meet up with a water buffalo, don't make eye contact, for heaven's sake don't criticize their horns, and immediately make a beeline for the Canary Islands (a herd of canaries are so much friendlier, feathers and all).

Without warning, our driver, who had momentarily slowed down, floored the Land Rover. Now don't miss this: think of a former agoraphobic who couldn't go to the store for peanut butter. And then he drove right through the middle of the buffalo herd. It was like something you see on television and you think, *No way. That didn't really happen. Must be trick photography.* Here I was, smack dab in the middle of this absurd adventure!

Had the driver said to me, "What do ya think, Patsy: Should I go for it?" I would have told him he would have to be out of his ever-loving mind to consider taking on a herd of wild animals. So I'm glad he didn't take a vote; the ride turned out to be a highlight of my trip. I mean, how many people can say they hydroplaned through a herd of stampeding water buffalo? It will look so good on my résumé.

Here's the best part. It happened so fast I didn't have time to work up a healthy case of panic. Besides, I was too busy bouncing my head against the inside roof while trying to watch the buffalo stampede on all sides of us.

The buffalo are probably still in therapy as I write this. "I dunno, doc. I was minding my own business, grazing on dinner when a white box full of wide-eyed creatures flew through the herd. Honestly, it took the curl right out of my horns."

Yahoo! A former scaredy-britches boot-scootin' over the savannahs of Africa . . . and loving it.

—*I Second That Emotion*

Cody the Canine Crackup

· patsy clairmont ·

You know what cracks me up? I have a grand-dog.

For many years, I could hardly wait to become a grandma; but trust me, I never considered the possibility of having a grand-dog. Nor had I ever been introduced to a Jack Russell terrier (alias Wacky Raucous Scarier) until our son's dog, Cody, came for an unescorted, extended visit. I didn't remember sending an invitation, but sure enough, he arrived at my doorstep wagging his tail behind him.

Did I say behind him? Let me restate that. Cody's breed, when on the defensive, points its tail skyward and vibrates it like a Geiger counter needle detecting a find. And while initially all that tail gyrating appears to be a friendly gesture, one soon realizes that Cody is announcing that your presence profoundly annoys him. To support his threatening effort, he adds a growling murmur, suggesting that the offending party should "back away now."

After just a short time together, Cody and I needed a therapist because our dysfunctional relationship was wearing me down. I tried to sway Cody's aggressive behavior with doggie treats, but he was unimpressed. I even fixed him an egg—with melted cheese, mind you. After I served it to him, he growled at me for standing too close to his dish.

Then I bought him a toy lion, to which he seemed to respond gleefully. But within three minutes, he dropped the now maneless lion at my feet. When I looked down, I saw he had also ripped off the lion's nose and pulled out the stuffing from the open cavity. Now, I could be reading into this, but this gesture felt like a direct warning: "Watch out, Grandma. You're next!"

Les and I usually retire around midnight. Customarily, Les slips into bed a few minutes before I arrive. (Girls have beauty regimens, you know.)

But A. C. (After Cody), when I would step out of the bathroom and head for my side of the bed, I would meet opposition. Cody had bonded with Les and had apparently decided that one of us could sleep near him, and it wasn't going to be me. With tail twitching and head down, Cody served up his deepest murmurings. Les had to repeatedly rebuff his guard dog so I could clamber into my own bed. The battle was on, and Cody was about to find out I could snarl too.

Early one morning, Cody indicated by ecstatic leaps that he wanted to go outside. So I told Les I would do the honors. I dragged my body to an upright position, slid into my slippers, and headed for the front door. In hindsight (no pun intended), I realized Cody wasn't indicating he needed to go outside. He was celebrating that he had already gone . . . inside. And what I first thought was unfeigned enthusiasm for me was actually his lauding his achievement in my face, or more accurately, on my foot.

The truth of his dastardly deed sunk in as I submerged my foot in a large, ahem, "deposit" that Cody had left on the hall rug. Not realizing I was foot-first in fresh deposit, I stepped onto the hard-wood floor and slid three feet to the front door. I howled as I slid, but I wasn't laughing. I'm not that enthused about mornings to begin with, so when you add stepping in dog doo to waking up at the crack of dawn, the statistical probability of me having a good day is not promising. (I'd tell you the exact numbers, but I've forgotten them already.)

Les, hearing my howl, came on the run, thinking Cody was once again threatening me. Instead, Les found me—miniature, gray-haired, and on all fours—growling at that fifteen-pound Oscar Mayer gonna-be.

Now don't get me wrong; Cody is cute. In fact, he's darling. But he certainly isn't cuddly, and he would never win Mr. Congeniality.

He's deliberately antisocial and purposes to maintain a short dance card.

Cody does have his moments when he will bound into my office carrying a toy and wanting to play, but his idea of "play" is for me to chase him around the house. Now, for the sake of relationship, I try. But quite honestly, I'm too cotton-pickin' old to be sprinting around couches, chairs, and tables in pursuit of a three-year-old puppy. Besides, my house can't take the jarring that my bounding creates; and for some reason, I don't take corners as gracefully as I once did.

When our grandchildren come over, Cody gets a full workout. But he is the instigator. Not long after grandsons bebop through my door, great shouts of glee reach the house rafters as riotous racers speed through the halls. Cody, who's always in the lead, has one of the children's toys firmly gripped between his molars, and he's grinning.

Cody loves stuffed animals, small plastic toys, and shoes. His goal is to gnaw them into oblivion. So far, he has shortened the neck of a giraffe, de-trunked two elephants, and put serious doubt in a stuffed lion that he is truly king. One thing I know for sure: Noah wouldn't have wanted Cody on the ark.

But Noah can't have him anyway—I don't give away family. Grandmas are like that, you know. I'm committed to this growling, gnawing, oversized gerbil of a dog . . . who makes me laugh daily. Unbridled enthusiasm is endearing, and Cody's breed, like Superman, can leap tall buildings in a single bound.

When I think about it, what are a few altered belongings between family members? And what clan doesn't have a few growlers in its midst? Besides, who but Cody would bound to the door each time I come home, genuinely glad to see me (at least initially)?

There's nothing like family!

—*All Cracked Up*

Horse sense is the thing a horse has which
keeps it from betting on people.

—W. C. FIELDS

My only pets are plants. I don't mind offering food and
water to any living thing on occasion, but every day?

—LUCI SWINDOLL

part four

Giggling in the Pews

Laughing Out Loud in Our Churches

The secret of a good sermon is to have a good beginning and a good ending, then having the two as close together as possible.

—GEORGE BURNS

Bloopers from the Church Bulletin

- The peacemaking meeting scheduled for today has been cancelled due to a conflict.
- The outreach committee has enlisted twenty-five visitors to make calls on people who are not afflicted with any church.
- The pastor would appreciate it if the ladies of the congregation would lend him their electric girdles for the pancake breakfast next Sunday morning.
- The audience is asked to remain seated until the end of the recession.
- Ushers will eat latecomers.
- During the absence of our pastor, we enjoyed the rare privilege of hearing a good sermon when J. F. Stubbs supplied our pulpit.
- Next Sunday Mrs. Vinson will be soloist for the morning service. The pastor will then speak on "It's a Terrible Experience."
- The concert held in the Fellowship Hall was a great success. Special thanks are due to the minister's daughter, who labored the whole evening at the piano, which as usual fell upon her.
- A song fest was hell at the Methodist church Wednesday.
- In the bulletin during the minister's illness: GOD IS GOOD Dr. Hargreaves is better.
- Bertha Belch, a missionary from Africa, will be speaking tonight at Calvary Methodist. Come hear Bertha Belch all the way from Africa.
- Remember in prayer the many that are sick of our community.
- Miss Charlene Mason sang "I will not pass this way again," giving obvious pleasure to the congregation.

- For those of you who have children and don't know it, we have a nursery downstairs.
- Barbara remains in the hospital and is having trouble sleeping. She requests tapes of Pastor Jack's sermons.
- Irving Benson and Jessie Carter were married on October 24 in this church. So ends a friendship that began in their school days.
- At the evening service tonight, the sermon topic will be "What is Hell?" Come early and listen to our choir practice.
- Please place your donation in the envelope along with the deceased person you want remembered.
- The associate minister unveiled the church's new tithing campaign slogan last Sunday: "I Upped My Pledge—Up Yours."
- Our next song is "Angels We Have Heard Get High."

The Lord's Prayer

(from the lips of babes)

Our Father, who does art in heaven. Harold is your name.
Our Father, who art in heaven, how didja know my name?
Our Father, who are in heaven, Howard be thy name.

An evangelist was praying to God one time and said,
"God, what's a million dollars to you?"

And God answered, "A penny."

So the evangelist said, "God, what's a million years to you?"

And God said, "A second."

So the evangelist said, "Well then God, wouldn't you please
just lend a penny to this poor servant?"

And God said, "Just a second."

Todd Wields the Sword:
His Own Story

· todd hafer ·

I'll never forget how the competitive tension hung in the air like smoke. The anxiety gnawed at my stomach, and the steely determination of my foes flashed in their eyes.

I had been practicing all week, working on every facet of my performance. I knew once the weekend came I had to be ready. I'd be up against fierce competitors—many crazed by steroids—firm in their resolve not only to defeat me, but to humiliate me as well.

Yes, those third-grade Sunday school sword drills were rough. What? You thought I was talking about my days as a high school football player? Get real. No coach was ever as harsh as Mrs. Klefcorn, and no gridiron battle was as fierce as those played out in the cold basement of Broomfield Baptist Church.

I can still envision Mrs. K. with skin—and a personality—like beef jerky, standing in front of our class. Her hairdo was the same height and density as the hats worn by the guards at Buckingham Palace, and in one hand she held a yardstick which she'd snap loudly on the craft table if we got too noisy. In the other hand, she held a big, black, intimidating King James Bible. For years the rumor had circulated that King James himself had given that Bible to Mrs. K., but it was never confirmed.

Mrs. K. would begin each class the same way. She'd set her jaw and rotate her head like a tank turret to ensure she had everyone's attention. Then the words would leap from her mouth: "It's time to drill! Swords in the air!"

Almost in unison, we would raise our Bibles high overhead. Then we would all lean forward, waiting for Mrs. K. to announce the first reference. I know that some of you probably participated in sword drills in which you had to find only a particular book of the Bible. I mean no disrespect, but such drills are for wimps. With Mrs. K., you had to find chapter and verse then spring to your feet and read it aloud.

On one particular Sunday, I arrived in class riding a two-week winning streak. But I was nervous. Timmy Waller was back from vacation in the Ozarks, looking tanned and ready. I knew his dad, a deacon, had probably held family devotions every day of their vacation. During his two-week absence, he'd probably heard most of the Bible read to him. The cheater.

Then out of the corner of my eye, I saw Judy Bittle, holding her dusty-rose petite KJV in her white-gloved hands. Another cheater. Those so-called fashion gloves virtually eliminated the slippage associated with sweaty palms. Judy had used this trick before, and I'd thought of filing a grievance with the Sunday school board. But Sparky Klein told me that while gloves were helpful in the gripping department, they could also reduce digital dexterity by up to 9 percent. So I had decided to keep my mouth shut.

My thoughts were shattered by Mrs. K.'s foghorn voice: "Matthew 6:19!" In a nanosecond, my Bible was open, my fingers flash-flipping through the pages. Habakkuk—dunder! Classic mistake. I hadn't opened far enough. Feeling the heat, I plunged forward. Epistles to the Romans—arrrgh! Too far! I backtracked. Ah-hah! Matthew at last! Now if I could just get to chapter six in time. Timmy and I shot to our feet in perfect unison. But he had made a fatal strategic error. While rising he had forgotten to keep his finger on the verse! *Maybe next time, loser!*

As he scanned the page in a panic, I was already reading, "Lay not up for yourselves treasures upon earth, where moth and rust doth corrupt, and where thieves break through and steal."

Mrs. K. smiled at me. Or at least I think it was a smile. It could have been gas. "Very well done, Todd," she said. "Timmy was close, but maybe he's missed just a wee bit too much Sunday school this month. Now, Todd, you may come up to the Bible Bounty Treasure Chest and claim your prize."

Lay not up for yourselves treasures upon earth, I recited in my head as I strutted to the chest. In compliance with the rules, I closed my eyes as I thrust my hand deep into the chest. Right away I felt something steel and grabbed it. Steel meant quality. Not like those cheap plastic disciples that broke the first time you played army with them. "Moth and rust, moth and rust," I hummed as I pulled out my prize and eyed it proudly. It was a bank shaped like the earth!

I lost that bank long ago, but I haven't forgotten Matthew 6:19 or my introduction to the concept of irony.

—*Snickers from the Front Pew*

Can You Help Us?

· author unknown ·

A man and his wife approach their pastor and ask for his help. "Our boys are always in trouble," they tell him. "We have tried everything, but they continue to break things, steal, lie, and generally cause trouble. Can you help us?"

The pastor agrees to talk to the boys. "Drop them off one at a time," he instructs the parents. The parents drop off the youngest, promising to return to get him soon. The pastor asks the boy to sit in a chair across from his desk.

After staring back and forth at each other for a few minutes, the pastor finally says, "Can you tell me where God is?"

The boy just sits there and doesn't answer.

The pastor, annoyed by the boy's refusal to respond, looks at him sternly and repeats the question louder this time. "Come on, son—answer my question. Where is God?" The little boy shifts in his seat, but still doesn't answer.

Losing patience, the pastor practically shouts, "I asked you a question, boy! Where is God?"

To the pastor's surprise, the little boy jumps up out of his chair and runs out of the office. Too frightened to wait for his parents, the boy runs all the way home, up the stairs, and into his brother's room. He shuts the door and pants, "We're in BIG TROUBLE. God's missing, and they think we did it!"

The sermon this morning: "Jesus Walks on the Water."
The sermon tonight: "Searching for Jesus."

What's the Matter with Johnny?

· author unknown ·

In Sunday School, Johnny heard how God created everything, including human beings. He seemed especially interested when the teacher said that God formed Eve from one of Adam's ribs. Later in the week, Johnny's mother noticed him lying down and clutching his side. She asked, "Johnny, what in the world is the matter?" Johnny replied, "I have a pain in my side. I think I'm about to have a wife!"

Potlucks: Not Always Good Fortune
· todd and jedd hafer ·

The "potluck" dinner is a tradition as old as the Jell-O mold itself. It has been a revered Christian tradition since churches moved from tents into buildings with electric ovens and indoor plumbing, and trust us, it will continue to be an important part of church life as long as leftovers lie brooding in parishioners' freezers.

In fact, to this day, our mom has a Deepfreeze full of stuff that's been frozen longer than Walt Disney. Every spring we urge her to throw out her many frost-covered Ziplock bags, but her reply is always the same: "I can't throw this stuff out. I'm saving it for the next potluck!"

We can't be sure of the exact origin of the potluck concept, but we did hear from a reliable source that it was the brainchild of a pastor who resided somewhere in the Midwest. It seems that one Friday night, he was struck with an inspiration: "Hey, my family members are the only ones who get to taste the worst food in our house! What fun is that? What if the whole church got together once a month and sampled the most horrific cuisine, the most cryogenically entombed leftovers from every household? It's crazy, perhaps even a little dangerous, but I think it could promote bonding within the congregation and provide a stronger sense of community—if it doesn't kill us first."

This gustatory epiphany quickly swept through the churches nationwide. And it came to pass that folks soon began arriving at church toting paper plates, twelve-pound tuna casseroles, enough Swedish meatballs to feed all of Sweden, and Jell-O sufficient to drown a woolly mammoth.

Churchgoers were encouraged to "come to the fellowship area

and enjoy the food, fun, and fellowship!" Long lines formed, children stuck their fingers into black olives and staged boxing matches. (These bouts, along with cock fights, are now illegal in most states.) Large adults wedged themselves into metal folding chairs and spilled instant pink lemonade on themselves. People laughed heartily, then asked suspiciously, "Who made the corn pone?" A tradition was born.

But just because the potluck is a sacred tradition doesn't mean it can't be improved or enjoyed more thoroughly by the savvy potluck goer. Here are a few tips to keep your potlocks from going to pot:

1. Add variety by sending your spouse or significant other out for pizza or chicken. Many people will thank you for this. We don't encourage you to put the take-out food in a casserole dish and try to pass it off as home cookin', but you probably won't invoke divine judgment if you fudge just a bit. Think of it as bringing a blessing in disguise:

"Hey, Marv, this chicken is down-home delicious. You fry it yourself?"

"Why no, an old army buddy of mine made it. Fella named Sanders. He's a colonel."

2. The brownies may look good, but they were actually prepared by a parishioner's eight-year-old daughter (probable name: Naomi) and taste exactly like small squares of sod.

3. You can never go wrong with macaroni 'n cheese if you throw in tiny squares of meat for protein's sake. One warning here though: it has to be the right meat. For example:

- Ham—good
- Hamburger—OK
- Spam—pushing it
- Recently thawed red snapper—not good

- Panda meat—very bad
- Anything that ends with the words "meat by-product"—induce vomiting

4. When selecting a little plate with a slice of cake on it, choose a corner piece. You get more frosting that way, and even an inept cook can't mess up frosting.

5. Eat the Jell-O early or it will liquefy, and you'll be sucking shredded carrots and banana chips through your teeth.

6. Never argue with Mrs. Swensen about her famous fifteen-bean salad. Case in point: "Mrs. Swensen, there aren't fifteen kinds of beans in the whole world! What kind of scam are you trying to pull?" "Yes, there are! Navy, kidney, lima, pinto, Mexican jumping . . . uh, jelly?"

7. Never eat Mrs. Swensen's famous fifteen-bean salad.

8. Clearly label all dishes. Once we mistook a potpourri center-piece for trail mix. It tasted terrible, but our breath did carry a lovely elderberry pine scent for the next week.

9. Make sure you pay attention to which cup you drink from. There's nothing worse than mistakenly grabbing some kid's cup and drinking eight partially chewed Cheerios and a Star Wars action figure in a thick saliva base.

10. Most important of all: Never, ever, ever bring devil's food cake, not even as a joke.

—*Snickers from the Front Pew*

The Oak Leaf

· *author unknown* ·

little boy was paging through the big, old family Bible. Suddenly, something fell out of the Bible, and he picked it up and looked at it closely. It was an oak leaf that had been pressed between the pages. "Mom, look what I found," the boy shouted. "It's Adam's suit!"

Just Say Thanks

· mark lowry ·

A few years ago I'd just finished a concert and was standing at the back of the auditorium when a little old lady walked up to me.

"That sure was pretty singing," she chirped.

I said, "Thank you, ma'am."

Suddenly, the woman's beauty-shop-blue hair was wiggling, her head was shaking so hard. "Oh, no, son," she corrected me, "don't thank me. Just say, 'Praise the Lord.' It wasn't you singing; it was God."

"Oh, no ma'am, it was me," I said. "God can sing a lot better than that."

When I traveled in college with the evangelistic team, every now and then a weightlifter would travel with us. He was one of these big, brawny, bold characters.

He used to tell the audience that he wasn't the one lifting weights, but Jesus in his tennis shoes. Some nights he couldn't get the weights up off the ground, and I'd lean over to our piano player and say, "Isn't that something? Jesus can't lift five hundred pounds!"

I heard a story once about a preacher driving through the hills of Virginia. He came upon a little old lady working in her garden on her palatial ranch. He noticed how every bush was beautifully manicured, how the sidewalk was perfectly edged. He told her what a beautiful place God had given her. She said, "Yes, he has. But you should've seen it when he ran it by himself."

Another time, I was standing with a friend of mine at Estes Park, Colorado, during the Christian Artists Association's "Singing in the Rockies." My friend was complimenting a very well-known Christian artist about a song he'd sung that week. This person said, "Oh, it wasn't me; it was the Lord."

I thought to myself, "Friend, it wasn't THAT good!"

You see, God, who one morning before breakfast, spoke the Word and previously nonexistent worlds began to spin, *can* lift five hundred pounds off the ground.

The Lord, who invented music, surely can outsing the angels and knows notes Beethoven never heard.

And so, no matter how good we are, we would be absolutely flawless if it were totally God doing it through us. Seems to me, then, it's senseless to say, "It wasn't me; it was God."

God gives talents. But just like the parable of the talents says, what we do with them is up to us. God may have given you a beautiful voice, but if it is going to improve, it's up to you. God may have given you a beautiful piece of land, but he'll never cut the grass or trim the hedges.

And have you ever noticed that most successful people are not always the most talented? Talents aren't worth much unless the owner of them keeps plugging.

And then, when you get those compliments, chuck the false humility and shock that little blue-haired lady. When folks tell you they enjoyed your singing or your sermon, your weightlifting ability or your green thumb, a simple thank you is what that person deserves.

—*Out of Control*

Bloopers from the Church Bulletin II

- A bean supper will be held on Tuesday evening in the church hall. Music will follow.
- Potluck supper Sunday at 5:00 PM—prayer and medication to follow.
- A cookbook is being compiled by the ladies of the church. Please submit your favorite recipe, also a short antidote for it.
- The Diet Club will meet Thursday night at 7:30 PM. Please use the large double door at the side entrance.
- Our annual church picnic will be held Saturday afternoon. If it rains, it will be held in the morning.
- The Ladies Society will be selling their new cookbook at the church supper this Wednesday night. The proceeds will help purchase a stomach pump for our community hospital.

The Exodus

· author unknown ·

Nine-year-old Joey was asked by his mother what he had learned in Sunday school. "Well, Mom, our teacher told us how God sent Moses behind enemy lines on a rescue mission to lead the Israelites out of Egypt. When he got to the Red Sea, he had his engineers build a pontoon bridge, and all the people walked across safely. He used his walkie-talkie to radio headquarters and call in an air strike. They sent in bombers to blow up the bridge and all the Israelites were saved."

"Now, Joey, is that REALLY what your teacher taught you?" his mother asked.

"Well, no, Mom, but if I told it the way the teacher did, you'd never believe it!"

The Glory of Gum

· marti attoun ·

Wrigley's announced that the company is investing millions of dollars on scientific research about the many health benefits of chewing gum, such as reducing stress.

The company could save a fortune by simply interviewing the real experts on the stress-reducing powers of gum: mothers. For at least one hundred years, mothers have been carrying emergency sticks of gum in their purses to buy themselves a little peace of mind. As soon as a kid has two baby teeth to grind together and can understand the words "spit it out in mama's hand," a mother begins unleashing the stress-reducing power of gum.

I speak from experience—having been on both the bribed and the bribing end.

As a seven-year-old, I quickly learned that nothing makes a boring sermon go down easier than a fat wad of sugary Juicy Fruit. Sunday mornings, Jana Sue and I would make a beeline to sit beside Jackie, an older woman whose purse seemed to hold an eternal supply of Juicy Fruit. There were few permissible distractions or sources of entertainment for kids in the pews. Thank heaven for Jackie's purse.

First, Jana Sue and I amused ourselves by studying the church bulletin, which was mimeographed on chalky white paper as thick as a paper plate. Sometimes the scent of the royal purple ink still lingered. Ever so quietly, we would crease and fold the bulletins into a paper airplane or a hat, using the Baptist Hymnals on our laps as our desktops. While creasing, we'd glance now and then with intent expressions at the preacher because he had an evil habit of plunking kids names right into the sermon if he thought they weren't paying enough attention, or worse, if they were being noisy.

"And that's you, Martha and Jana Sue, that God is talking to . . ." he'd shout. Such words could stop a kid colder than Opal's spinach-and-tuna casserole at the church supper.

Bulletin folding could be stretched into four minutes, unless a nearby adult clamped a hand over the activity. Another distraction was studying the members of the flock for signs of new perms or dresses and guessing how long it would take before Viola nodded off and got nudged in the side by her husband. Sometimes there'd be some unexpected excitement, such as when one of the old deacons put an arm around his old wife's shoulder.

We'd make little churches with our clasped hands and steeples with our index fingers and twiddle all the people inside. We'd fiddle with the offering envelopes and flip open our Bibles and check out the illustrations for the hundredth time.

Then, just when we thought we couldn't stand another second of sitting still and we'd never survive until the final amen, Jackie would come to the rescue.

Jana Sue and I would watch as Jackie's hand slipped quietly to the shiny patent-leather purse on her lap and silently unhooked its clasp. She wouldn't make a sound as she reached inside and pulled out two perfect lovely yellow sticks of Juicy Fruit.

Her eyes never left the preacher as she placed the gum into our eager outstretched hands. Neither did ours as we slipped the gifts from their foil wrappers and counted our blessings.

Adventures at Church Camp

· mark lowry ·

In the summer of 1973, like every other summer, I went to church camp. In fact, that year I was even leading the singing. "Beulah Land"—that was its name—was outside of Nacogdoches, Texas, and our church owned it. Beulah Land was a running camp. That's because my church was a "running" church.

We had changed churches by then, from one Baptist church to another, that is. My daddy didn't like the way our old church was teaching that we'd have to go through the Tribulation, because he didn't want to go through the Tribulation. So we moved.

The choice had come down to two churches, and the winner was the one that shouted the most. My dad was tired of a dead church. He wanted a shouting church, even though he never shouts. He wanted one that had some life to it, and he got it. Our new church was a shouting, and sometimes a running, Baptist church. When I say shouting, I'm not talking about speaking in tongues. Their shouting was in English. And their running, well, I don't know what that was. But they'd shout, and when they got excited, they would just take off running.

Sometimes I took off running just to get out of the service.

That worked especially well at church camp. That's why I called it a running camp. You get that many kids together and tell them it's okay to run around during the church service, you're going to see some running all right.

Of course, it was still your basic church camp in the things that really mattered. Powdered eggs. Separate swimming hours for boys and girls. Ugly leather crafts.

And pranks.

There are traditions to uphold at church camps.

Even running, shouting Beulah Land Baptist church camps.

One of my best time-honored pranks dealt with glass-vial stink bombs. (Helpful hint: Quality stink bombs are available at novelty shops and magic stores everywhere. I always carry a spare; you never know when you might need a good stink bomb.)

A bunch of guys and I would wake up in the middle of the night and go over to the girls' dorms. All the girls' dorms had window air conditioners. What the girls didn't know was that because of the way the units fit into the window, there was just enough room in the bottom left corner to poke a pair of pliers—holding a stink bomb.

The best part was that, before the bomb had done its work, we could be back in bed watching the lights in the girls' dorm flip on and the girls in their nightgowns rush outside.

And, invariably, you could always hear someone say, "Was that Mark Lowry?!"

I got blamed for everything (or credited, however you want to look at it).

But during all the prank-pulling, running, shouting, and song-leading, I got saved.

We had two services that night. We had two services every night. My brother got saved in the first service, and I got saved between the two services.

I had whittled off my thumbnail that week. I was whittling, turned my thumb the wrong way, and phewt! I whittled that thumbnail right off. The camp nurse put a curler on it. I remember the first song I sang after I got saved was "The Lighthouse." I "thank God for the lighthouse," and I raised that curler to heaven.

I was talking to Debbie, this deaf friend of mine, after the first service. She was reading my lips by the light of the lamppost.

After I told her how I didn't think I was saved, she said, "Let's pray."

Well, she started praying first. And she kept right on praying—and kept on praying. Since she's deaf, and she had her eyes closed, I thought, *I can't pray until she shuts up. The Lord could come before she quits praying and I'm gonna be left.*

Finally she stopped, and I got right with God.

There was a slight problem, though. I was already supposed to be saved. I had joined the church years before. I was the leader in my youth group, for crying out loud. So I thought people would laugh at me since everyone took for granted I was already saved. But they didn't; they were happy.

I've gotten saved many times since then, to tell you the truth. J. D. Summer says something pretty smart: "God saves me every day."

When you think about it, we are being saved every day of our lives. I don't believe you can be born again and again and again, but, boy, it seems like you can.

A good title for life would be: *How to Become a Christian Now That You're Born Again.*

Know what I mean?

But it was real at church camp that night, and things have been different ever since.

Almost everything. While everyone was happy for my spiritual encounter, it sure didn't keep them from blaming me when things kept happening around the camp.

For some reason, when the girls in their nightgowns kept running out of their dorms in the middle of the night, swatting at the stinky air, we still heard, "Was that Mark Lowry?!"

(Well, God saves you, he doesn't ruin you!)

—*Out of Control*

Church choir members were putting on a car wash to raise money for their annual tour. They made a large sign which read:

CAR WASH for CHOIR TRIP.

On the given Saturday, business was terrific, but by two o'clock the skies clouded and the rain poured, and there were hardly any customers.

Finally one of the girl washers had an idea. She printed a large cardboard poster that read:

WE WASH and GOD RINSES!

Business was soon booming.

The Workman's Hymnal

· author unknown ·

Dentist's Hymn: "Crown Him with Many Crowns"

Contractor's Hymn: "The Church's One Foundation"

Baker's Hymn: "I Need Thee Every Hour"

Weatherman's Hymn: "There Shall Be Showers of Blessings"

Ophthalmologist's Hymn: "Open My Eyes That I Might See"

Tailor's Hymn: "Holy, Holy, Holy"

IRS Hymn: "All to Thee"

Shopper's Hymn: "By and By"

Teacher's Hymn: "Be Still and Know"

Church Basketball:
Throwing Up a Prayer

· todd and jedd hafer ·

A long time ago, someone decided that a little sweaty competition among church congregations would be healthy, fun, and spiritually enriching. Shortly after that idea was dismissed, someone else came up with the concept of "church league basketball."

A church basketball league is just like a regular league, except that the players are in poorer shape and have to come up with creative expletives like "sugar! golly-darn!" or "great gallopin' googly-moogly" when they miss a shot or fire a chest-pass into a teammate's groin. Some churches have gyms in which they can practice. Others, like Broomfield Baptist Church, practice in the driveway with a twelve-degree slant and a crooked nine-foot basket with no net.

But BBC does have the Hafer Boys—four strapping young men (we were always getting strapped for something) eager for some holy hoop-la. Since we are all well over six feet—except for one brother who for the sake of example we'll call Chadd—we are expected to play starring roles and lead the team to the league championship.

Unfortunately, while we have talent for folding bulletins and lip-synching hymns, we don't exactly play like Doctor J. In fact, we play more like Doctor Quinn, Medicine Woman. We take comfort, however, because no one else in the church league can play either—except for those Assembly of God cheaters who always bring in several ringers.

After one of these seven-foot behemoths does a 360 slam-dunk on us, we all mutter, "Sure, that guy goes to their church! Nobody who can jump that high even goes to church! He's close enough to God already!"

But we don't want to give the impression that we've been sore losers. Sure, we've been sore. And we do lose—plenty. But we've always enjoyed the competition, especially the one year we made it to the finals. That was the year Jedd shot up five inches over the summer. (Chadd shrank about one and a half inches over the same span, but cumulatively speaking we gained some key net height.)

The season began beautifully. We creamed the Catholics, pounded the Presbyterians, mauled the Methodists, and edged the Episcopalians. But our winning streak was snapped at the hands of the Agape Ranch (aka the cheaters we mentioned earlier). We simply had no chance. Their team was composed of athletic Bible college students and no old fat guys. This was in direct violation of the unwritten code of church league basketball: Every team must have a minimum of two old fat guys, preferably with corrective lenses and at least one knee brace per geezer.

Anyway, we rebounded from our defeat and breezed through the rest of the season right into the post-season tournament finals. There, of course, we met Agape again.

Fortunately for us, one of our aged, hefty guys with thick glasses—for the sake of anonymity, we'll call him "Dad"—had a wedding to perform and couldn't make the big game. So, with our chances enhanced, we set about the business of lovingly beating the soup out of these upstart Bible students with their neat little haircuts and forty-inch vertical jumps.

It was a close game. Back and forth. Neck and neck. A barn-burner right down to the wire—and many other sports clichés too numerous to mention. The score was tied 44 to 44 with eight seconds to play, and we had the ball. The crowd, all seventeen people, were on the edge of their seats. Todd lofted a perfect pass to Dave, a deacon with eleven kids and a mean outside jump shot. As the clock ticked down to one second, Dave lofted a desperation shot from the top of the key.

The shot was on line. It arched poetically into the stale air of the Broomfield Community Gymnasium and Bingo Hall. All eyes followed the leather sphere as it went straight into the buck!

No, that's not a typo! The ball stuck fast in the antlers of a giant trophy deer head that peered down from the wall above the backboard. The deer stared menacingly at us as if to say, "You may have shot me, made my body into jerky, and mounted my head up here, but I have your lousy basketball! You stinkin' Bambi killers!"

Of course the game stopped right there, "dead on the wall" so to speak, since that was our only basketball. As we pondered our situation, Dad walked into the gym with grains of wedding rice sprinkled in his hair. He looked at the scoreboard, then at the buck.

"It appears," he said, "that we're on the horns of a dilemma."

Dave spoke up, "I don't mean to be disrespectful, Pastor, but I think that's actually a deer, not a dilemma. Them dilemmas, they got short, curly horns and live in Australia or the Ozarks or somethin'."

We all looked at Dave in wide-eyed bewilderment—even the deer. Then the conversation returned to which team should be crowned league champions. The Agape-ites claimed they should get the first-place trophy because they beat us in the regular season. We, of course, pooh-poohed that approach, arguing that when playoff time comes you can throw the regular season right out the window. Dave quickly pointed out that the gym didn't have any windows.

Dad stroked his chin for a moment before plucking a grain of rice from his hair and nibbling on it thoughtfully. Then with Solomon-like wisdom, he spoke, "Well, this dilemma—I mean situation—reminds me of something from the Old Testament."

He strolled to the scorer's table and lifted the handsome chrome-plated trophy, which featured an eight-inch hoopster frozen in mid-jump shot. It was quite striking. "Tell you what I'm gonna do," Dad began. "Since both of you want this precious trophy so much, let's just cut it in half. That way each team can share the glory. Sure, the trophy will be grotesquely disfigured and forever a monument to both teams' selfishness, but that's just fine with me. If neither side can give a little here, I see no other recourse."

Of course we Hafer boys could see right away that Dad was going for the Solomon-and-the-baby principle. He fully expected his boys to do the right thing and set an example of humility and grace that would be remembered as long as out-of-shape Christians gather in musty gymnasiums to battle on the hardwood.

Dad smiled at us knowingly. "So, guys, what should I do? Give this trophy to Agape or go get the hacksaw?" The trophy case at Broomfield Baptist Church is small. There's a bowling plaque, some perfect-attendance certificates, and one third-place ribbon from the 1973 all-church tug-o'-war. There isn't really enough room for a whole basketball trophy in there anyway.

But half a trophy fits just fine. And thanks to the fact that we shrewdly chose "heads" rather than "tails" in the ensuing coin toss, we got the half of the guy that's holding the basketball! Sure, we know what you're thinking: *Isn't half a trophy somewhat unwieldy?* Okay, it toppled over on the bowling trophy a few times, but we quickly discovered how to prop up our half-hoopster with a twenty-two-ounce can of creamed corn.

Next season, we plan to win a whole trophy. You see, some of those guys from Air Agape are graduating from Bible college and being called away to the mission field. Far away. Whereas the nucleus of our team works at a local feed store. They aren't going anywhere—especially Dave, who's still trying to get his GED and pass his driver's license test.

So the undisputed championship should one day be ours...if we can find a stick long enough to free the basketball from the buck's antlers.

—*Snickers from the Front Pew*

Divine Call

· author unknown ·

The pastor's church was called Almighty God Tabernacle. On a Saturday night several weeks ago, the pastor was working late and decided to call his wife before he left for home. It was about 10:00 PM, but his wife didn't answer the phone. The pastor let it ring many times. He thought it was odd that she didn't answer, but decided to wrap up a few things and try again in a few minutes. When he tried again she answered right away. He asked her why she hadn't answered before, and she said that it hadn't rung at their house. They brushed it off as a fluke and went on their merry ways.

The following Monday, the pastor received a call at the church office, which was the phone that he'd used the Saturday night before. The man he spoke with wanted to know why he'd called on Saturday night. The pastor couldn't figure out what the man was talking about. The caller said, "It rang and rang, but I didn't answer." Then the pastor remembered the mishap and apologized for disturbing him, explaining that he'd intended to call his wife.

The man said, "That's okay. Let me tell you my story. You see, I had been very depressed and was planning to kill myself on Saturday night, but before I did, I prayed, 'God if you're there, and you don't want me to do this, give me a sign right now.'"

The man continued. "At that point my phone began to ring. I looked at the caller ID, and it said, 'Almighty God.' I was afraid to answer."

You Couldn't Be More Wrong . . .

· author unknown ·

1. Anna Baptist was the wife of John the Baptist.
2. Paul used the King James Version of the Bible.
3. Noah's wife was Joan of Ark.
4. Pharaoh refused to let the Children of Israel leave Egypt until Moses gave him ten plaques.
5. Moses climbed Mount Cyanide, met with God, and brought back the Ten Commandments.
6. Unfortunately, Moses died before the Children of Israel reached Canada.
7. The fifth book of the New Testament is called the "Axe of the Apostles."
8. The Epistles are the wives of the Apostles.

On the Road and in the Air

Laughing Out Loud at Our Traveling Adventures

*The journey of a thousand miles begins with a
broken fan belt and a leaky tire.*

—AUTHOR UNKNOWN

Accidental Perspective

· patsy clairmont ·

I bounded out the door, energized because I had completed a writing project and motivated by a purchase I was going to make. I had been working on a story for two days, and it had finally come together. While I was writing, in the back of my mind, I kept thinking about a used piece of furniture I had seen in town that would be just right for my office. I needed a book and display case, and this piece offered both, plus more. The price was right, too.

I was excited as I headed into our little town full of delightful shops offering wonderful "deals." I was almost to my destination when, in my rearview mirror, I noticed a car coming up behind me at a fast clip. I remember thinking, *That guy is going to hit me if I don't scoot out of his way.* I added a little pressure to the gas pedal and turned my wheel to hurry into a parking space. That's when it happened. A loud thud was followed by crunching, scrunching, grinding sounds as my minivan rearranged the front fender of a parked car.

I am of the belief that if you're going to hit a vehicle, you should select one with someone inside. When you smack an empty, parked car, you pretty much rule out the chance the other person may have been at fault. All eyes are focused on you. Also, if you must have an obvious accident, it's better not to do it on Main Street in your hometown.

I jumped out of the van and ran over to look at the smooshed car. The victim's vehicle had two silver beauty marks streaking down the side, and the chrome fender curled out instead of in, giving it a flared appearance.

Then I ran inside an office and asked if the car belonged to anyone there. It didn't, so I headed for the next building, when I heard someone call my name.

A lady I had just met at Bible study two weeks prior waved and ran across the road in my direction. She gave me a hug and told me everyone in the ladies' dress shop heard me hit the car and came to the window to see what had happened and who had done it. When I had stepped out of my van, she had squealed and announced, "I know that woman!" In a small town, anonymity is difficult.

Then she added as she checked out the crumpled car, "You could tell this story at conferences."

Trust me—at that point, I was not eager to tell my husband, much less the world, what I had done.

I dashed into the shop where the bookcase was and called to the clerk, "I have to go turn myself in at the police station, but would you please measure the bookcase for me? I'll be right back to purchase it."

As I headed for the front door, I heard a sweet voice say, "I just sold it."

"No!" I exclaimed. "You don't understand! I hit a car in my attempt to get here and buy this piece," (as if that would make a difference). Then I whined, "The buyer wasn't driving a dark blue Buick, was she?"

The saleswoman assured me she wasn't. I could tell she felt bad about my situation, but I felt worse. On the way to the police station, I thought, *Maybe I'll have them throw me in the slammer and sleep off this trip to town.*

When I arrived, I confessed to a woman behind a barred glass window that I had committed a crime. She called for an officer to come and write a report. While I was waiting, I noticed the zipper on my pants was down and my red shirttail was sticking out like a road flag. I quickly turned away from the men sitting in the waiting area to "fix" myself and tried not to think about how long my red tail had been waving. A fleeting recollection of me looking like Wee Willie

Winkie as I ran from one store to the next, trying to find the car's owner, darted through my head.

The officer appeared and began to ask questions. Near the end of the inquest, he asked, "How much damage did you do to your vehicle?"

"I don't know," I answered.

"You don't know?" he echoed.

"I don't know," I validated.

"Why don't you know?" he pushed.

"Because I didn't look."

"Why didn't you look?" he asked in disbelief.

"I'm in denial," I confessed.

"You have to look," he told me. Then he sent me out to get my registration.

I returned, paper in hand.

"Well," he said, "how much damage?"

"Sir, I didn't look," I said with polite resignation.

He shook his head and gave me back my registration. As I was leaving, I heard him say, "You'll have to look."

When I got home, I asked Les to go out and look.

It turned out I had swiped her car with my running board. The board wasn't off, yet it wasn't on. It was neither here nor there but suspended in air. Threads at each end dangled the board precariously.

Afterward, I realized that when we spend too much time looking in our rearview mirrors, we may hit something right in front of us. Looking back is an important part of conscientious driving, but it's not the only safety precaution.

Likewise, it's important for us to benefit from our past, but we don't want to get so struck staring at yesterday that we collide with today in a destructive way.

Unlike the situation with my van, I can't send Les to check my past and assess how much damage was done. That's my responsibility.

As the officer said, "You'll have to look." But once I take care of what I can do to repair the past, I then need to drive on, benefiting from occasional rearview references and perspective.

—*Normal Is Just a Setting on Your Dryer*

The Sunday school teacher was describing how Lot's wife
looked back and turned into a pillar of salt when little Jason
interrupted. "My mom looked back once, while she was
driving," he announced triumphantly, "and she turned into
a telephone pole!"

Location, Location, Location

· mark lowry ·

I used to sit in the back of the plane.

Know why?

Because I have never seen a plane back into a mountain.

Have you ever seen a plane wreck? The whole plane will be demolished and that tail will be sticking up. I figured if I got my tail on the tail, I'd save my tail.

Then I started getting a little braver and began moving up.

Now, I always get as close to the front row as I can, so if the plane crashes, I'll be killed and not maimed.

I was sitting on the front row the other day, and there was an old lady sitting next to the window. I knew she was old because her teeth were brand-new. She was sound asleep, in one of those coma kind of sleeps. You know, drooling on her pillow.

That's how you know you've had a good night's sleep—when you wake up and have to wring the pillow out in the morning.

Watching her drool, I had this awful urge come over me to just slap the side of her chair and holler, "WE'RE CRASHING!" But I didn't do it, and that's how I know God is still working in my life.

But before I got brave enough to be on the front row, I made it to the exit row.

On the exit row, you've got more leg room, and—an extra special incentive—they don't let children sit on exit rows.

The one thing that bugs me about the exit row is The Seatback Card. The airline attendants are always coming by to say, "Have you read the seatback pocket card?"

Have you ever noticed those cards? In big letters, it says at the top, "If you cannot read this, then please tell the attendant."

What it says in a nutshell is, if the plane goes down I've got to know how to open that door and help people off the plane.

Did you know that? If you sit on the exit row, that is your responsibility. You've got to know how to open the door and help people off the plane.

I always tell them, "Yeah, I've read it. I'd be happy to stay on the burning plane and escort others off. 'Thank you for flying Delta. Thank you. Watch that first step, it's a doozy!'"

Help people off the plane? I'll help them off the plane. If they can follow my wide rear end going through that door. I may put a flashlight between my legs that they can follow. But, baby, I'm getting off the plane!

—*Out of Control*

The Joys of Business Travel
· kathy peel ·

Sometimes I amaze myself. I have an uncanny ability to get into desperate situations, especially on business trips. Here's a case in point. After a full day of book promoting, I finished my last television spot in Denver. As I hurriedly packed my autumn dog-and-pony show for my coauthored book, *A Mother's Manual for Holiday Survival*, it crossed my mind that I resembled part of the road crew from Ringling Brother's Circus. I thought about professional women who travel with a laptop computer and leather briefcase. Instead of a portfolio of important papers, I travel with five bags full of fall squash candle holders, a new-potato wreath, decorated pumpkins, hurricane lantern, pomegranates, fall leaves, pine cones, and pilgrim hats filled with popcorn and candy corn. I lugged my bags to the rental car knowing I'd best get to the airport fast or else I'd miss my plane.

I climbed into the unfamiliar car and found the windshield wipers, radio, defroster, air conditioner, hazard light, and hood release before finally locating the headlights. When I turned the ignition key, the seat belt closed around me like an Indiana Jones booby trap. (I have a few choice words for the idiot in Detroit who invented those belts.) I hate being at the mercy of a high-tech car. To make matters worse, I didn't have a clue as to how to get to the airport, and I only had forty-five minutes to get there.

About that time, a Federal Express truck pulled up in front of me. Ah . . . who else would better know the streets of Denver, I thought. I'll use the old damsel-in-distress approach. After a five-second hair fluff, lipstick touch-up, and squirt of perfume, I made my move. As the car withdrew its tentacles, I jumped out and approached the driver. "Excuse me, sir." I used my most helpless feminine voice, "I wonder if you could tell me how to get to the airport?"

Unimpressed with my charm, he hardly glanced up, then answered in one breath, SureTakeEleventheasttoBroadwaythengo northtwoblockstoColfaxtoUniversitytheneastonMLKandfollowthe signs . . . you can't miss it." He jumped in his truck and sped off to make his next delivery deadline.

"Okay, Kathy, you have a college degree," I said to myself. "No problemo." I took off.

After traveling eight blocks, the reality of my situation hit. Trust me, you don't know fear until you've been in a strange city after dark, driving a rental car during rush-hour traffic in a snowstorm, only to find yourself in the adult-only district of downtown not knowing whether you're getting closer to the airport or farther from it.

Spotting a policeman two lanes over, I dodged a patch of ice and two lanes of traffic to chase him down. I pulled in front of his patrol car and stopped at a red light. Wondering what moving violation I could commit, I thought, *What have I got to lose? A jail cell would be safer than where I am right now.* I leapt from my car and ran back to the police car and asked for directions. He spurted out a few highway numbers then pointed at the green light to remind me I was holding up fifty cars. I ran back to my car, jumped in, and sped off. Involuntarily I took the scenic route and arrived at the airport three minutes before my plane was scheduled to take off—only to learn it had been delayed. Thanks to the snowstorm in Denver and tornadoes in Dallas, I could now sit down and have a coronary at leisure.

I would be remiss at this point if I didn't share my deepest feelings about flying: It stinks. After experiencing more than my share of planes dropping a few thousand feet in midair, hitting thunderstorms that cause dinner to land in the aisle, and engines overheating at thirty-three thousand feet, I've decided I don't like being anyplace higher than I can jump from and land comfortably. But since my career dictates that I travel two to three times a month, I've been forced to create a number of defense mechanisms to deal with my fear of flying. I have been known to rip shirt sleeves off of businessmen seated next to me, leave fingernail claw marks in the vinyl armrests, and make a complete fool of myself trying to find someone in the cabin who will listen to me talk nonstop through the flight so I forget I'm in the air. I didn't figure out until we landed that a lady who listened to me all the way from Dallas to Kansas City once didn't speak a word of English. (I thought she was totally enraptured with my life story since she nodded and smiled for an hour and a half.)

On this particular snowy night, I sat alone. As I recapped my day, I thought about how, in spite of flying, I really do love my work. What a privilege!

—*Do Plastic Surgeons Take VISA?*

With all the discounted fares, the airlines are coming up with new ways to make money. For example, it now costs $3.50 for your kid to ride the baggage conveyor.

—JOE HICKMAN

Overbooked

· author unknown ·

While sitting in the upper deck business class front seat of a Cathay Pacific 747 in Taipei, the following announcement was heard over the cabin PA system:

"Ladies and gentlemen, we are overbooked and are offering anyone $1,000 plus a seat on the next flight in exchange for their seat on this flight."

After a short pause, the offer was loudly accepted by someone in the cockpit.

Another Town, Another Trauma
· sheila walsh ·

During my years as a youth evangelist in Europe, I slept in some pretty strange places. Usually, I stayed with local church members who were kind enough to open their homes to me. No matter where I stayed, I appreciated the kindheartedness of those who took me in. But I have to tell you, some of those places left me a bit traumatized.

One day, I went home with a couple who seemed very nice and almost normal. As we pulled into the driveway of their home, I listened, but not a bark or a purr could be heard. This was good. It's usually the pets who push you to your limit.

After supper the lady asked me if I minded sleeping in the garage. I said that was fine, assuming they had converted it into some sort of bedroom. But the man of the house pulled his car out of the garage and unfolded a camp bed in its place. It was November in England and very cold. I put on more clothes to go to bed than I had on during the day. Every thirty minutes the freezer would start up and chug, chug till I longed for a cat to put in each ear.

In the morning, as I lay there stiff from cold and discomfort, the husband started his car to go to work, and all the exhaust came flooding in. I thought, *I bet they're closet atheists, and they're trying to kill me!*

I stayed with another family in Holland for a week. They spoke no English, and I spoke no Dutch. The family shouted at me the whole time, apparently thinking it would make it easier for me to understand them.

I have lots of fun stories to tell and laugh about in the comfort of my own home. But every story is held together by the common thread of God's faithfulness through it all. He was my constant companion.

—*Overjoyed!*

The policeman couldn't believe his eyes when he saw the woman drive past him, busily knitting. Quickly he pulled alongside the vehicle, wound down his window, and shouted, "Pull over!"

"No," she yelled back, "they're socks!"

Where's Your Drive?

· martha bolton ·

I don't believe age should be a determining factor in issuing a driver's license. One's driving skill, reflexes, and knowledge of the highway laws are what should be held up to scrutiny. Age is nothing more than a number.

At the age of seventy, my mother scored 100 percent on her driving test. She was an excellent driver who preferred to drive in the slow lane whenever possible. When making left turns, her motto was "If you wait long enough, it'll eventually be clear." Having to drive the streets of Los Angeles, this motto often kept us waiting at intersections into the night, but Mother was emphatic. Whenever risk could be avoided, she avoided it.

The rules of the road have changed so much lately, I wonder if she'd even pass the test today, much less get another perfect score. Remember the good ol' days when the potential answers to a question like "What do you do when someone is tailgating you?" used to be: (a) slow down, (b) swerve to avoid his hitting you, or (c) gently honk your horn? There wasn't any (d) draw a gun on him, or (e) pull over and beat him to a pulp.

The test is more difficult because of so many societal changes, but as I said, age shouldn't be a determining factor in driver's license renewal. If, however, any of the following apply to you, you might want to consider voluntarily surrendering yours.

It Might Be Time to Give Up Your Driver's License If . . .
- You've ever waited in an intersection through three or more light changes before making your left turn.
- You consider the raised median your personal driving lane.

- You've ever worn out a new brake light on a two-mile trip to the store.
- You refer to going thirty-five miles per hour as "flooring it."
- You've ever honked at a pedestrian and said the words, "Move it, buddy! You think you own the sidewalk?"
- A tractor has passed you on the freeway, and it was being pushed.
- You've ever used a stoplight to get in a short nap.
- You've ever made more than three U-turns within a single block.
- You've driven for more than twenty-five miles with your left turn signal on.
- You've ever tried to report a fire truck for tailgating you.

—*Didn't My Skin Used to Fit?*

Hurry Up, We're Going to Be Late

· *joey o'connor* ·

I was flying down the freeway.

No, Jimmy, I wasn't a happy camper.

My wife was not making me happy. You had to be there. Like a raving, Gumby-eyed lunatic at the controls of an intercontinental Concorde jet ready to snap the exploding whip of the sound barrier, I VAAROOOM-DAHed down the cow pasture-lined highway at over one hundred miles an hour. On the wrong side of the road. With the pink rental car speedometer tickling 107, nothing was moving faster than this Hertz hurricane of fury except my eyes, looking everywhere at once for Barney Fife to pull me over.

Clutching a pathetic, wrinkled rental car map, I precariously balanced the steering wheel in my left hand while attempting to read the microscopic words and squiggles directing me to the car rental return area. Blood surged through my veins as my anger spiked at the thought of a British mapmaker laughing at silly, frantic Americans careening into smelly cow fields while trying to read the extra-fine print.

"Uuuggghhh," I screamed as I locked my leg onto the accelerator and launched a series of stammered outbursts audible only to the empty passenger seats, "WE'RE-GOING-TO-MIIISSSS-THEEE-PLA-AA-A-NE!"

Maybe I was temporarily going insane? Maybe I ate some bad British burger and had contracted the "Mad Cow" disease?

No way. This wasn't my fault.

My wife, Krista, and mother-in-law, Betty, were at the Heathrow International Airport terminal where I had dropped them off fifteen minutes earlier.

It was the end of our London vacation and I was doing my best Clark Griswold impersonation.

An hour earlier, I was told we were going to spend "just a few minutes" at the Laura Ashley shop in downtown London. Just real quick.

"You wait in the car," they told me.

Laura Ashley-Smashley-Mashley.

I waited. That was my first mistake.

"Just a few minutes" turned into an hour as Krista and Betty oohhed and aahhed over floral prints, elegant sweeping dresses, mommy-and-me matching outfits, bedspreads, wallpaper, curtains, stationery sets, toilet roll holders, Prince Charles earwax removal kits . . . you get the picture.

Three times I sounded the five-minute warning.

Should've called James Bond.

A handsome 007 would have stolen their attention.

Should've called Henry VIII.

Didn't Anne Boleyn shop at Laura Ashley?

Now I was a lost Mario Andretti wannabe fumbling over fouled-up directions, doing God only knows how many kilometers per hour, while coaching myself in the fundamental driving techniques of the Motherland, "Stay to the *left* of the road. STAY LEFT. STAY LEFT."

The plane was leaving, not boarding, for America in fifteen minutes.

Bingo. Finally found the car return. Stormed inside and was warmly greeted by a cordial British car rental return manager who queried, "Might you be Mr. O'Connor? I just received a phone call from your wife who's wondering where you are."

Visualize rage.

After silently simmering on a shuttle bus slower than a late-afternoon English tea, I bounded off the bus and through the electronic doors at the main terminal. Standing next to an x-ray security station,

Krista and Betty waved me down and yelled their only foreign words of the whole trip, "Hurry! We're going to miss the plane! What took you so long?"

Excuse me? Did I just hear what I just heard? What took ME so long?

Mother, daughter, and the fang-bearing American Werewolf in London son-in-law dashed through the first security station where polite British officers scanned our Laura Ashley bags and checked for terrorist bombs. We sprinted twenty paces only to be halted again by a second security station.

"Why are there so many x-ray machines?" Krista said out loud. "We're never going to make the plane!"

That was it—I snapped. "Krista! This! Is! Not! The! United! States! Of! America! We are in a foreign country where bombs explode eh-ver-ree-hee day!"

When the smoke finally cleared, my claws retracted and the three of us began running toward our gate through a marathon series of hallways. Our gate, #1,851, was the last gate, the farthest away from the curb, about as close as you can get to the border of the former Soviet Union.

Dressed in wool sweaters, thick overcoats, and long everything for the nip of English weather . . . plus, loaded down with—yes, you got it—Laura Ashley dresses, Laura Ashley kids' clothes, Laura Ashley power tools, sweat poured down our faces as we half-ran, half-speed-walked down the labyrinthine hallways of Heathrow International Airport.

In my mind, anger bubbled and popped in a thick, meaty stew. *Fine. This is just fine . . . I hope we miss the stupid flight. I don't care one bit. I hope, I hope, I hope we miss the plane.*

Bumbling along, I looked at the sweat-drenched faces of Krista and Betty. They both looked back at me and went ballistic in side-splitting laughter.

Reciting the polar opposite of what I was thinking, they launched another volley of laughter and screamed, "We can make it! C'mon ... keep going! We can make it!"

Tears streamed down Krista's and Betty's faces as they cried all the louder at the sight of the tortured scowl on my mug. Open mockery.

Funny. Real funny. Laughter as a defense mechanism, right?

Finally, we arrived at our gate and were met by an airline attendant wildly waving her arms.

"Hurry, they're going to shut the airplane door," she cried.

Huffing, puffing, perspiring, almost expiring, we boarded the airplane. A flight attendant stopped us in the aisle and apologized, "I'm sorry, but your seats in Coach Class were taken. We had to bump all of you to First Class."

Krista's eyes lit up like landing lights and met my bloodshot, narrowed slits. Tilting her head to one side, she beamed in surprise. "See, isn't it a good thing we were late?"

—*Women Are Always Right and Men Are Never Wrong*

You've got to be careful if you don't know where you're going, because you might not get there.

—YOGI BERRA

A young woman, discovering her seat was by the window, pleaded with the flight attendant to move her to a seat on the aisle.

"You don't understand," she said. "I'm going to be in my cousin's wedding, and I don't want to mess up my hair."

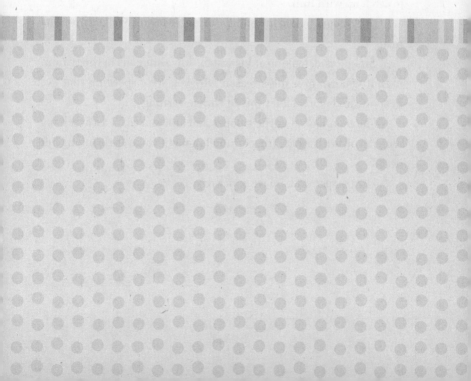

Quick Thinking

· author unknown ·

There was a middle-aged guy who bought a brand new Mercedes convertible SLK.

He took off down the road, sped it up to 80 mph and enjoyed the wind blowing through what little hair he had left on his head. He accelerated some more, then looked in his rearview mirror. A trooper was right behind him with blue lights flashing and siren blasting.

"I can get away from him with no problem," thought the man, so he floored it and flew down the road at over 100 mph.

Then he reconsidered. "What am I doing? I'm too old for this kind of thing."

He pulled over to the side of the road and waited for the trooper to catch up with him.

The trooper pulled in behind the Mercedes and walked up to the man.

"Sir," he said, looking at his watch, "my shift ends in thirty minutes. If you can give me a reason why you were speeding that I've never heard before, I'll let you go with a warning."

The man looked at the trooper and announced, "Last week my wife ran off with a state trooper, and I thought you were bringing her back."

The trooper said, "Have a nice day."

Driving Advice

· mark lowry ·

I got another ticket the other day. It wasn't for speeding. It was for running a red light. I was stopped at the light, then I made the mistake of looking in my rearview mirror.

There sat a policeman.

Oh no, I thought. *He's going to see I don't have my seatbelt on.* So without thinking—and I have no idea why—I stepped on the gas.

I blew right through that light. Right in front of that surprised cop.

He pulled me over.

"Did you realize you just ran that red light?" he said.

"No, I didn't." And that was the truth. I was too busy thinking about my seat belt.

"Didn't you hear all those people honking at you?" he asked.

"Yes," I answered.

"Well?" he asked.

"Well," I said, "I didn't think much about it because I know a lot of people around here."

He didn't much care for that answer, because he started writing a ticket right away.

It reminded me of the time I got a speeding ticket in Dallas. The officer asked me if I knew why he stopped me.

"You don't know?" I asked. "Well, I don't either."

—*Out of Control*

Murphy's Laws of Driving

· joe hickman ·

- No matter where you park your car, the sun will be shining on the driver's seat when you return.
- There is always room to merge behind a diesel bus.
- If you try to change lanes to get off the ramp, the car in the lane to your right will speed up.
- Trucks that overturn on the highway are always filled with something sticky.
- When you move to the next lane because it's going faster, it becomes the slowest lane.
- The guy with a bumper sticker that says "If you can read this, you're too close" always tailgates.
- The first bug to land on your windshield will splatter right in front of your eyes.

—www.HaLife.com

Life with Momo

· luci swindoll ·

Humor punctuated my grandmother's life. Whether her words ended in a period, comma, semicolon, question mark, or exclamation point, laughter was her punctuation of choice. She died in her eighties, which was way too soon for me, because her life was a guiding light of joy. I miss her still.

As a young woman rearing four children, my grandmother laughed with life and taught her kids to do the same. When my brothers and I were youngsters, my mother often treated us to stories about her own childhood with "Momo" (that's what we called my grandmother), and without exception, laughter was part of the telling. Even in sadness or difficulty, Momo found moments of comedy.

For example, one Sunday night during church, my grandfather was called out of the service to go with a police officer to the scene of a car accident involving several vehicles on the outskirts of their little Texas town, El Campo. Being a justice of the peace, Granddaddy often dealt with matters of law or public decorum regarding local citizens, most of whom he knew personally. Momo couldn't bear not knowing what happened, who was involved, whether anyone was hurt, the location of the pileup, and everything involved with the accident, but she wasn't asked to go with them.

Being hopelessly nosy, the minute church was over, Momo grabbed the children, marched out to the family car, asked a friend to drive her (she never drove a day in her life), and headed straight for the scene of the accident. This was in the early 1920s, so car ownership was more or less at a premium. Even the smallest fender bender was front-page news. All the way there, Momo was coming up with different scenarios, trying to figure out what happened, putting together in her mind various pictures of what it looked like, all of which were based on her own imagination.

The truth was, Momo knew nothing about cars. She didn't know make or model or year or any information of value. All she knew was color. You'd ask her, "What kind of car does Mr. Grant drive?" and she'd answer, "Blue."

When they pulled up to an area where lights were flashing and police cars had gathered, it was indeed a mess. Four cars had smashed together on a dirt road, two of which had overturned and landed in an open field. Momo asked to be let out immediately so she could find out what happened and whether anyone was seriously hurt.

Stepping out, she headed straight into the fray as her friend drove the car with her kids to the other side of the pileup to get out of the way of vehicles arriving. After looking around awhile and learning that no one was seriously hurt, Momo walked through the wreck and came to the very car in which she had arrived. Then she leaned in the window and in all seriousness asked, "Can you folks tell me what happened here tonight?"

Her kids nearly died laughing and said, "Mother, get in the car. It's us!" To the sound of raucous shrieking, she crawled in the back-seat, and the car literally shook with laughter.

—*Life, Celebrate It!*

Church Van
(Unsafe at Any Speed)
· todd and jedd hafer ·

We'll never forget the Sunday that a new family joined our congregation at the Broomfield Baptist Church. Our dad, the pastor, announced with great gusto that the time had come—we now needed a church van, and he had found a great buy.

It took us a while to warm up to the idea of a church van, especially this one. Its exterior was two-tone—seafoam green and off-seafoam green. The front seat, captain's chairs, had been re-covered in traffic-cone orange vinyl. The second- and third-row seats were their original avocado color. (Or maybe it was off-off-seafoam green.) The floorboards may or may not have been carpeted. We're not sure because from almost the very beginning, they were littered with cola cans, donut boxes, and a coffee-stained road map of Nebraska.

On the positive side, the van did have a great sound system—an eight-track tape player. And we had a selection of three, count 'em, three tapes from which to choose.

There was *Foghat Live*, which came with the van. There was an Evie tape, purchased for us by the Proverbs 31 Tuesday Night Bible Study and Macrame Guild. We're not sure of the title, but it's the one that had the song "I'm only four-foot-eleven, but I'm going to heaven and that makes me feel ten feet tall." They don't write 'em like that anymore. And, for the rare over-sixty-five passengers, there was George Beverly Shea's Greatest Hits, which we won from the Lutherans in a wallyball match.

As far as we know, the van, which we eventually named Van Morrison, was never serviced. The engine sounded a lot like a trash compactor. Also, only Dad and a 300-pound elder named Chet were strong enough to budge Van's manual transmission; and, even with their strength, it took much grinding and gnashing of gears.

There was another reason that Dad was about the only person who could or would drive Van——the inside rearview mirror was broken off. Dad was trying to adjust it one time, and . . . well, he is a power lifter. He tried to stick the mirror back on the windshield, but there are a few things that even Elmer's glue and lots of hollering won't fix. He did the next best thing, though. He propped the mirror up on the dashboard, wedging it carefully between a hymnal and a crumpled 7-Up can. After the mirror popped into his lap a few times, he used some of Mom's flannelgraph Old Testament characters to ensure a more snug fit.

Given Van's many problems, we'd often suggest, "Hey, Dad, don't you think we should have this thing checked out? Maybe fixed up a bit?"

"Nah," he'd reply thoughtfully. "You see, kids, a van is a lot like eschatology. It's big and mysterious and you really shouldn't poke around in it too much. You just hope things will work out for the best." At this point in our conversations, we'd all grow quiet and nod our heads. (We had no idea what eschatology was.)

Van had some other minor problems. The speedometer needle was busted. Dad tried to fix it by taping a toothpick to the little orange stub of the needle, but the heavy vibrations from Van's engine always shook the toothpick loose and into the garbage on the floorboard. So we devised a method of guessing our speed. We'd stick our hands out the window and wait for a bug to hit.

If the bug-to-hand impact was mild, like catching an infield pop fly during a church softball game, we'd deduce that Van was doing twenty to thirty miles per hour. If a bug made a loud snap when it hit and stung like a high-five from Muhammad Ali, we'd guess fifty miles per hour. If the bug felt like a white-hot bullet and made us scream like a twelve-year-old girl at an Osmond Brothers concert, we'd put the speed at seventy-one miles per hour and beg Dad to slow down. (By the way, if your speedometer breaks, try this method. Of course, your estimated speed may vary, depending on what kind of bugs are crowding your area roadways.)

Van's gas gauge was one of the few things that did work properly. But that didn't matter much. The little needle was rarely above the "E" line. You see, after buying his daily dirigible-sized eclairs, Dad usually had only about fifty-eight cents for gas. So we often used the "coast and pray method" of getting around. This method is surprisingly effective. We often rambled for twenty or thirty miles after Van's gas tank was as dry as Margaret Thatcher's sense of humor.

Our most memorable trip in Van occurred in 1983 when Dad drove the whole youth group up into the Colorado mountains for a week-long camp called "God's Li'l Survivalists." The idea was to get closer to God by living in tents and eating tree bark and stuff. Obviously this wasn't the kids' idea. In fact, when the needle dipped below empty twenty miles from the camp and Dad said, "Okay, start praying, kids," none of us did. We just bowed our heads and wondered what tree bark tasted like.

About five miles from our destination, Van planted himself firmly in the middle of the dirt road and refused to coast another foot. "No problem," Dad said cheerfully. "I'll just get out and push. Todd, you and Jedd steer. It'll be a good workout."

Dad had little trouble pushing the hulking "Mean Seafoam Green Machine." Unfortunately, we weren't as successful with the steering wheel. After we killed two innocent aspen trees, Dad had to switch plans. He got in the van to steer, and we pushed. We made it about a mile—maybe. It's hard to judge distance when every muscle in your body is screaming in pain and you see white spots jitterbugging before your eyes.

At that point, we abandoned Van and hiked the rest of the way to camp. Relief washed over us when we saw the crude log-cabin lodge that served as camp headquarters. The relief vanished when we saw the sign in the front window:

Welcome to Camp!
Next Week's Theme: God's Li'l Survivalists.

Dad has practically memorized the whole New Testament in Greek. But with dates, he sometimes has a few troubles. So he may have gotten things confused, but we decided to blame the confusion on the church secretary since she took the fall for most of the problems anyway.

After that fiasco, the elders decided to sell Van and try carpooling. And, hey, if you're the one who bought Van, please give us a call. Mom needs her flannelgraph characters back—the ones Dad used to prop up the rearview mirror. Mom has an awful time telling the "Fiery Furnace" story in Sunday school without Shadrach and Abednego. "Mrs. Hafer," some kid will always scream, "did the other two dudes get toasted in the furnace?"

"No," she replies, trying hard to hide the irritation in her voice. "They're on mirror duty in a really ugly van."

—*Snickers from the Front Pew*

part six

A Mind Is a Terrible Thing to Waste!

Laughing Out Loud at Ourselves

*My math deficit is pitiful. If my salvation were dependent on
adding a column of figures and getting the right answers,
I would need to take out fire insurance for my future.*

—MARILYN MEBERG

Crafty

· patsy clairmont ·

I do crafts. No, wait, that's not quite right. I own crafts. Yes, that helps to bring into focus the blur of materials stuffed into assorted baskets, drawers, and boxes in my attic and basement.

My craft addiction has left partially done projects pleading for completion. I have snarls of thread once meant to be used in needle-point and gnarly-looking yarn intended for an afghan. I have how-to books worn from my reading and rereading of the instructions. (I love reading; it's the doing that bogs me down.) Swatches of material, florist wire, paint brushes, grapevines, and (every crafter's best friend) a glue gun—along with a myriad of additional stuff—greet me whenever I open my closet.

Every time I'm enticed into purchasing a new project, I think, *This one I'll do for sure.* I've attempted everything from oil painting, floral arranging, quilting, and scherenschnitte (the German art of paper cutting), to quilling.

Quilling? you ask. For those of you unfamiliar with it, this craft requires you to wind itsy-bitsy, teeny-weeny strips of paper around the tip of a needle. Once they're wound, you glue the end, using a toothpick as an applicator so your paper coil doesn't spring loose. Then, with a pair of tweezers, you set your coil onto a pattern attached to a foam board, securing it with a straight pin. You are then ready to start the paper-twirling process over again. To be a good quiller, it helps if you, the crafter, are wound loosely. I believe quillers (at least this one) have to be a few twirls short of a full coil to attempt this tedious art.

You may be wondering how many of those paper tidbits one needs to finish a piece. That depends on the size of your pattern. I chose a delicate little snowflake. Taking into consideration that I'm a beginner (which is still true of every craft I've ever tried), I decided to select a small pattern and not overwhelm myself. (This would be like saying, "I think I'll go over Niagara in a barrel rather than a tub in hopes I won't get so wet.")

When I started my snowflake, I thought, *I'm going to make one of these for each of my friends and put them on the outside of their Christmas packages.* After five hours and a minuscule amount of noticeable progress, I reconsidered. *I will give these only to my best friends and include them in their gift boxes.*

A week later, I realized I didn't have a friend worth this kind of effort; only select family members would get these gems. And they would be all they'd get. I thought I would also include a contract for them to sign, agreeing to display their snowflakes well lit, under glass, in a heavy traffic area of their homes, all year.

Fifteen hours into my little winter-wonder project, I decided this would be the first and last paper wad I'd ever make . . . and I'd keep it for myself. It could be handed down in my family, generation after generation, in a time capsule, after my passing. I often wondered who the flake really was in this venture.

I suppose you're asking yourself, *Did she finish it?* Not yet, but I plan to (great inscription for tombstones).

I once attended a retreat where I was persuaded to join a wooden angel craft class. The angel done by the instructor (art major) as an example was adorable. Mine (craft minor) looked like an angel that might join a motorcycle gang.

Even that angel didn't get completed, because they ran out of heavenly parts. She had only one wing and was minus her halo. Actually, it was kind of sad. Today my fallen angel lies at the bottom of a box in my basement, covered with rotting quilt pieces and plastic ivy, still waiting for her ordination. May she rest in peace.

I took a painting class for credit and received an A. Finally, something I could succeed in! Of course, if that was true, why didn't I have a picture to hang?

It hit me that I didn't have a painting anyone could identify, much less display. For one of our projects, we painted apples in a bowl. When I took it home, my friend thought it was a peacock.

I approached the instructor and asked how I had earned an A in her class. "For showing up every week," she responded. She must have the gift of mercy.

Les and I started hooking a two-foot-by-three-foot rug twenty-five years ago. We're almost to the halfway point. We figure, in a joint effort, that we have hooked less than an inch a year and should complete it in the year 2012. You may want to get on our gift list.

I seem to be more into ownership than completion . . . and then I feel guilty. I've noticed I'm not alone in that. Some kindred spirits could stuff a landfill with their forsaken artistry. I wonder if that's why we have so many garage sales and so much garbage in this country. We sell off and throw away our unfinished business, and then we go buy more.

What happened to the notion "waste not, want not"? That's a great line. I wonder how it would look in cross-stitch? Oops, there I go again.

—*Normal Is Just a Setting on Your Dryer*

Did you know that all these have been demonstration sports at the Winter Olympics?

- Bandy (like ice hockey with a ball)
- Ice stock sport (a German variation on curling)
- Skijöring (skiing behind horses)
- Sled-dog racing
- Snowshoeing
- Speed skiing
- Synchronized skating (just as enthralling as synchronized swimming!)

These sports have been discontinued:

- Live pigeon shooting (really?)
- One-hand weightlifting
- Duelling pistol event (our personal favorite). This event required competitors to shoot (from 20–30 meters) at mannequins dressed in frock coats with bull's eyes on their throats! (Can anyone say, "YIKES"?)

My Olympic Suggestions

· andy andrews ·

Several weeks ago, I realized that for the first time in my life, I was not interested in the upcoming Olympic games. Having always been a huge fan, I wasn't sure if my indifference was due to the "China" factor or the realization that my short-term goals do not include stopping to watch television for two weeks.

However . . . when the swimmers got started, I was hooked. The whole Michael Phelps story was terrific, and I really enjoyed Rowdy Gaines' presence on the broadcast. Rowdy, a former "fastest swimmer on the planet," and I had several classes together in college, and he is a great guy. When the Phelps mini-documentary revealed that Michael consumes 12,000 calories per day, I remembered what it was like to eat lunch with Rowdy when he was pursuing his own swimming gold medals—he won three in 1984. Swimmers can really eat!

My family has enjoyed the "beach" volleyball events even more than the indoor version of the sport. Austin and Adam have become huge fans of 6' 9" Phil Dalhausser, aka The Thin Beast! Wouldn't you hate to play the net against *that* guy???

Doing a brief bit of research on the Olympic movement, I found some interesting facts:

1. There are 302 Gold Medals up for grabs in Beijing. Most of them are in sports you and I have never tried, and a great number are in sports we will never watch.
2. Synchronized Swimming (which is ridiculous to me) is the only Olympic event that *requires* makeup and hair gel.
3. According to the Olympic's own Web site, Judo is the only

Olympic sport where "submission holds *allow* choking an opponent or breaking an arm." Sheesh!

There are obviously some sports that never see any television time because very few people care to watch.

1. Trampoline? I see as much of this as I need to see. Our neighbor's kids are bouncing on one all the time.
2. Fencing? I'd rather watch someone *build* a fence.
3. Dressage? It's horse dancing—and the horse does all the work!

My own suggestions for new events include:

1. Cross-Country Ballroom Dancing
2. The Javelin Catch
3. 100-Meter Blindfolded Dash
4. Full-Contact Whining (I already see a lot of this in my line of work.)
5. Here though, is my greatest offering . . . 10-Meter Platform Cannonball. The medalists would be determined by a computer graphics display of the athlete who displaces the most water above the surface of the pool—in other words, the biggest splash. This would make television ratings history. Think about it. Would you leave the room as Japan sends a sumo from the 10-meter platform? I didn't think so.

—*www.andyandrews.com*

Rats Giggle

· marilyn meberg ·

This morning I read this headline in the newspaper: "Rats Giggle, Test Finds." A researcher at Bowling Green State University found that rats are not only playful, but they also love to be tickled. Of all creatures on the earth, in my mind rats would be the least likely candidates to take giggle breaks. I have found myself smiling about that fact all day. The article has also caused me to spin off on a reverie concerning "least likely" humans I have either known or briefly encountered whom I wondered if a smile, giggle, or laugh ever escaped their frozen lips.

Eighty-year-old Mrs. Davidson falls into the frozen-lip category. Yet, as a child, I found her fascinating. A good part of my fascination was undoubtedly that she would occasionally shout out disagreements during my father's preaching. I, on the other hand, wasn't even allowed to interrupt during second-grade reading group, much less Dad's sermons. I was tremendously envious of all she got away with.

Since she lived within walking distance of our parsonage, I loved dropping in on her. She never seemed particularly glad to see me; instead, she appeared indifferent to my visits. She had an acre of land on which she housed a number of chickens, a goat named Bert, and a cow also named Bert. (I never thought to question the duplication of names or the appropriateness of a cow having such a moniker.) Mrs. Davidson was always puttering around outside doing various little chores, and I trailed along behind her chatting and trying in vain to engage her in some way.

One night at supper my parents quizzed me about why I liked visiting Mrs. Davidson. I think they were concerned she might find me a nuisance or that she might hurt my feelings. I told my parents I liked her animals and loved the smell of her few bales of alfalfa, but more than that, I wanted to make her laugh. Both parents put down their forks and looked kindly at me.

"Honey," my father said, "I've never even seen Mrs. Davidson smile, much less laugh."

One of the things we did as a small family of three was make various bets. Dad was always betting my mother about some academic subject that he was sure he was right about, only to find he was totally wrong. That never seemed to squelch his enthusiasm, however, and the bets continued as long as they lived.

Thinking I might get in on the betting game, I said to my parents, "I'll bet I can get Mrs. Davidson to laugh before I'm in the third grade!" Rising to the challenge, they agreed and said they hoped I won the bet. Mom asked what kind of payoff I wanted.

"French toast for breakfast every Saturday morning for six weeks," I said without hesitation.

For at least a month I tried every conceivable thing I could think of to make Mrs. Davidson laugh. I told her jokes, I told her all the bad things Lester Courtney did in school, I even did acrobatics for her. No response.

Then one day, as I was heading up the path toward her messy property, I was attempting to perfect my imitation of how Mr. Brownell walked. Mr. Brownell had caught his leg in a threshing machine at some point in his life, and the accident resulted in the most memorable walk I'd ever seen. Whenever his weight landed on his bad leg, his whole body would veer dangerously out of balance. But somehow the flapping of his arms caused him to catapult in the opposite direction until everything appeared to be back in order. His head moved in perfect rhythm to all this disjointedness. It was quite a feat.

I had been working on this imitation for some time purely for my own sense of accomplishment. My efforts were interrupted by the sound of what could be likened to a donkey's braying. It grew louder and louder until finally I located where the noise was coming from. Mrs. Davidson was leaning against the side of her chicken house, laughing. She laughed so long, so loud, and so hard it made me a little nervous. It seemed to me making that much noise could kill a person.

"Well, Mr. Brownell," she finally gasped, "how nice of you to visit me," and then she went into another braying episode.

When I triumphantly announced to my parents that I had won the bet, they were concerned the laughter had come at the expense of another's misfortune. I explained that I had been working on the walk for weeks but never to be used for Mrs. Davidson, and in fact, I had no idea she saw me until I heard her laugh. Apparently convinced that my heart was not cruel, I was rewarded with French toast every Saturday for six weeks.

I still find myself wanting to make people smile or laugh. It's a little game I play with myself when experiencing a gloomy waitress, bank teller, store clerk, or any other frozen-lipped personage. It sure beats tickling rats.

—*Overjoyed!*

Most Dedicated to the Task

· patsy clairmont ·

I remember walking through the mall once when I noticed a quarter on the floor. Had it been a penny, I might have passed it by. But a quarter? No way. I stooped down and swooped my hand across the floor to scoop up the coin, but it didn't budge. I tried again. I could hear laughter coming from a nearby ice cream shop, but I didn't look because I was focused on the shiny coin. I tried to pick it up again, but it held fast. I tried prying it with my nails, I even took out my emery board and used it like a crowbar, trying to dislodge this gleaming coin.

As I stared at George Washington's immobile silhouette, I thought I saw him smirk. Then I realized George was not alone. The laughter nearby had grown to unbridled guffawing. I looked up and realized five teenagers were watching me and laughing at my financial struggle. It was the kind of laugh that told me they knew something I didn't.

"Okay, what's the deal?" I asked.

One girl confessed they had glued the quarter to the floor and had been watching people try to pick it up. The kids dubbed me the "most dedicated to the task." I giggled with them as I thought about my 25-cent antics.

—*Normal Is Just a Setting on Your Dryer*

You're as Young as You're Ever Gonna Be

· anita renfroe ·

I can't believe the stuff I drop money on in the cosmetics department of Walgreens. It's that no-questions-asked return policy they have that lures me in. It makes me feel I can be a fearless shopper when it comes to makeup and toiletries. Did the shade of lipstick you chose resemble the safety cones on the roadside when you got it home? No problem. Walgreens will take it back. Did the bubble bath promise to send you into bath-time nirvana but leave you with a rash instead? No problem. Walgreens will take it back. I've had some great fearless purchases, and I've had some real doozies.

I actually bought something called "Weight Reducing Cream" in a lovely pearlescent tube. Right there on the tube is printed, "Lose Pounds and Inches" and "Controls Appetite, Increases Metabolism, Firms and Flattens." Honey, if there was something in a tube that could do all that, wouldn't *you* trot it right up to the counter and lay down your hard-earned dollars? I had visions of myself actually losing weight while sleeping or—even better!—losing weight *while* eating dinner. If we live in the era of land rovers on Mars, could simultaneous eating and losing weight be too farfetched?

Well, I got the stuff home, popped the top, and just knew I was going to be firmed and flattened by daybreak! Wasn't Oprah just gonna call me right up and ask me to be on her "Amazing Transformations" segment in a week or two? Maybe I should dig out the digital camera and take some "before" pictures just in case.

According to the directions, I was supposed to rub a quarter-size dollop onto my tummy and "other problem areas" one hour prior to eating. (Don't they know that at a certain age, they're *all* "problem areas"?) So I slathered a good palmful onto my "areas" (everything between my boobs and my knees), reasoning that if a quarter-size dollop were good, wouldn't *seven* quarters be better? I felt sure that I would shrink before I got to REM.

Problem is, I never actually got to sleep that night. I felt exactly like I had overdosed on Sudafed as I flopped like a chicken on the rotisserie all night long. I was trying to sleep but felt like a live wire still hooked up to the power plant. After three exhausting hours of this, I got up in the middle of the night with heart palpitations, certain I was having some sort of cardiac incident, and tried to read the ingredients. Only then did I notice the fine print: the actively absorbed agent was none other than caffeine. I had smeared the equivalent of fifteen cups of coffee on my "problem areas." In this product's defense, I did lose weight from the bed gymnastics.

I believe that there's not much a girl won't do if the promise includes holding back the hands of time or erasing the marks that time has already made on her. I know I'm susceptible to the miraculous cream claims and the appeal of youth. But isn't the definition of "young" getting a good bit more youthful every year? Supermodels are told that their careers are over at the ripe old age of twenty-five.

It is hard to help my teenage daughter navigate this profoundly shallow culture. When every other television show is built around the premise of surgical enhancements and "extreme makeovers," it's a chore to convince a girl of any age that beauty is something deeper than a plastic surgeon can touch and that she radiates true beauty every time she shows love and compassion. (I wonder why we never see a TV show about that.) But I have come to a place of some acceptance in my life via the thought that no matter how old I feel, I'm as young as I'm ever gonna be. Think about that carefully: you will never be any younger than you are at this moment. Hello!

Age is relative anyway. For instance, if you are eighteen and it is your destiny to be taken from this life at the age of twenty-one, you may think you're young, but in reality most of your life has already been lived. That makes you old. On the other hand, if you are fifty-eight and you are going to live to be a hundred, you're young (proportionately). The point is, none of us knows how long we might live or how old that really makes us, so why not celebrate how young you might be? As Satchel Paige said, "How old would you be if you didn't know how old you are?"

I have known some aged people who are very young inside. Marge Caldwell from Houston is a vibrant sprite of a woman who sparkles and giggles when she talks and is going on ninety years young. She is a woman who knows that age is just a number on a driver's license. Conversely, I have known some teenagers and college students who by virtue of the weight of life upon them seemed as if they were very, very old.

This notion of today being my youngest day of the rest of my life makes me want to try to turn cartwheels, live a little more daringly, celebrate everything with a bit more gusto, and fully appreciate the gift of life. So today I will skip the caffeine body cream and maybe call a friend as I pour a second cup of fresh-brewed java.

Youth is not in a number or in a night cream or in a surgeon's scalpel. It's in your head and your heart. Be as mature as you must, but refuse to be any older than you are. Don't let this youngest day of the rest of your life go by without a little celebration!

—*Purse-Driven Life*

Near-Death Experience

· *author unknown* ·

A 54-year-old woman had a heart attack and was taken to the hospital. While on the operating table she had a near-death experience. Seeing God, she asked him, "Is my time up?" God told her, "No, you have another 43 years, 2 months and 8 days to live."

Upon recovery, the woman decided to stay in the hospital and have a face-lift, liposuction, breast implants, and a tummy tuck. She even had someone come in and change her hair color and brighten her teeth. Since she had so many more years to live, she figured she might as well make the most of them. After her last operation, she was released from the hospital. While crossing the street on her way home, she was killed by an ambulance.

Arriving again in front of God, she demanded, "I thought you said I had another 43 years to live! Why didn't you pull me from out of the path of the ambulance?"

God replied, "I would have, but I didn't recognize you."

Lord, Did You Misunderstand?

· natalie grant ·

My curtain call was quickly approaching. I was on tour with several different bands, and as the only female, I had a dressing room completely to myself. I wanted to look my best that night, so I had spent a little extra time getting ready, pulling on the cutest pair of jeans, tall stiletto boots, and a sassy little black leather hat. Right before I headed out the door, I prayed the prayer I always pray before facing the stage lights: "Lord, be glorified through my music, and may the words of my mouth and the meditation of my heart please you."

My band members took their respective places, then I waltzed into the spotlight, smiling my brightest smile and eager to get started. It was going to be a good night. I could feel it.

As we started the first song, I could hear the enthusiastic roar of the five thousand people in the audience. Each face seemed to be filled with warm encouragement, and the crowd's expectant energy filled the auditorium. The groove my band was laying down felt great, and I was belting out "Keep on Shining" at the top of my lungs.

Then I fell off the stage.

Yes, you read that correctly. *I fell off the stage!* I don't know exactly what went wrong. I had done that set of music many times before and always managed to stay on my feet, but somehow, this time was different. I'd like to blame the incident on one of the floor monitors—a speaker that plays back the sound of the band and my voice so I can hear what's happening. But the truth is, those monitors were in the same spot on the stage where they always were, and the one I tripped over certainly didn't jump out in front of me. But for some reason, on the last note of my first song, I walked right into it, lost my balance, flipped through an aerial movement that surely would have scored at least an 8 in any Olympic competition, and tumbled off the stage into the crowd.

At least part of me landed in the crowd; the other part was still dangling from the stage.

Fortunately (at least for me—the folks I fell on might not have felt so fortunate), people were standing right up against the platform, and they caught me. Otherwise I would have fallen right on my head. If I had been thinking, I could have pretended to crowd-surf, although I've never been one for mosh pits. (Okay, I've moshed in my mind many times but have never been quite cool enough to act it out.)

I guess the production crew had never seen an artist take a dive off the stage before, because none of them seemed to have a clue what to do. Finally the lighting engineer turned off the stage lights, probably hoping to diminish the sight of me sprawled between the edge of the stage and my human safety net. Thoughtfully, those kind people pushed me back up on the stage, where I lay for a moment curled up in the fetal position, probably thinking, *Lord, is there any chance you misunderstood when I asked that you would be* glorified *through my performance tonight? Maybe you thought I said* horrified?

I had been using a corded microphone, and as I went down, the mike went hurling into the crowd. Still lying on the stage but now hunched up like an armadillo, I pulled on the cord, yanking it in like a fishing line caught on a rock. Then I just lay there on the stage another moment, lost in the darkness, ready to burst into both tears and laughter at the same time.

Girl, you've got two choices, I told myself. *Get off the stage while it's still dark and never show your face in Ames, Iowa, again, or get up and keep going.*

I got up.

I had injured my ankle in the fall, but the real injury was to my pride. Although I was embarrassed, humiliated, insecure, and unsure of myself, I finished my show. Some of the other artists on the tour helped me up onto a stool. My injured ankle made it difficult to stand, so I took off my stiletto boots and finished the rest of my set in my socks. I was just thankful they were clean. Then I looked down and saw my pinkie toe peeking out of a small hole . . .

—*The Real Me*

Haircut Standards for the Armed Forces:

- Marines: Heads will be shaved.
- Army: Stylish flattops for all recruits.
- Navy: No haircut standard.
- Air Force: Complete makeovers as seen on the Jenny Jones show.

Hair Today, Gone Tomorrow
· sheila walsh ·

*I*f God counts every hair that falls from our heads, he must be exhausted counting mine with all the abuse I ladle out to my head of hair. I think some women have an extra gene called the "hair coloring gene." We poor souls honestly believe we can buy a little box of color in a drugstore, and we will look like the woman pictured on the box. Never happens!

But that doesn't stop me. Oh, no! I march on down the road of hair destruction in search of that elusive perfect shade.

My first foray into this bleak and unforgiving world was with a shade called "warm coffee brown." *Sounds lovely*, I thought. *I like coffee . . . This will be good.*

It turned out black. Boot-polish black. Elvira black. A crow-died-on-your-head black. *Never mind*, I consoled myself. *I'll try again.*

And so I did with "golden ash."

How emotionally evocative, I mused. *I'll be like a tree in the fall, all shades of gold and amber.*

Well, I was half right. I did look like a tree . . . in the middle of June. It was green, green, green.

I pressed on. Next I ordered what was described as "luxurious hair" by a woman on television with big hair. I thought, *I can't go wrong with this. I just attach these hairpieces under my own hair for full, flowing, glorious locks.*

When I opened the box, the contents looked like a row of dead hamsters. I tried them on and had to admit I resembled a rather sad-looking cocker spaniel.

But the greatest damage I've ever done to my hair happened when I was eighteen years old and just about to leave my little

Scottish town for university in the big city of London. I was very excited and wanted to look hip. I had long, silky hair, which I decided was too old fashioned. I needed a new look. So I bought a Vogue magazine and studied all the pictures. One model had hair that was cut in layers and softly permed. She looked beautiful.

"Do you like this hairstyle, Mom?" I asked one evening after dinner.

"It looks lovely, Sheila," she replied. "Why?"

I decided not to look until the hairdresser was finished. I wanted a big surprise. I got one. At first I thought something was wrong with the mirror, but then I realized I was looking at my head. I can't adequately depict the fright that was me. My hair was layered different lengths on each side. It was also fried. I looked as if I'd stuck my wet finger in an electric socket. I numbly paid and began to walk down the road.

I talked to myself as I went, "It's not as bad as you think. It'll be better when it's washed. Christ may return today."

Just at that moment I spotted my mom and my brother, who were waiting for me outside a coffee shop. Stephen was laughing so hard he was clinging to a pole to try to hold himself up. My poor mother was attempting to make him stand up and behave, but her efforts just caused him to laugh harder. He ended up lying on the sidewalk.

I was eighteen then. I'm forty-two now, and thankfully I've learned how to handle my hair. One other thing I've learned is that my worth to God has nothing to do with how I look or feel. He is committed to me on my good hair days and on my bad hair days. And when I make a fright of my spiritual life—even committing errors that seem "permanent"—Jesus can wash them away. He is eager to do so and will never laugh, regardless of how ridiculous I look.

If today, as you look in the mirror, you wonder if this is a face only a mother could love, remember, it's a face a *Father* loves!

—*Overjoyed!*

You've reached middle age when all you exercise is caution.

—AUTHOR UNKNOWN

The trouble with jogging is that by the time you realize
you're not in shape for it, it's too far to walk back.

—FRANKLIN JONES

I Dare You

· luci swindoll ·

More often than not I wish I had taken a camera along to capture some of the zany antics of Marilyn and me. Then maybe people would believe they really happened. However, the story I am about to relate is one of those rare occasions that I will be forever grateful no camera was available to record.

I had been living in Southern California for about a year when I received a call from a former Mobil Oil supervisor in Dallas; he was going to be vacationing in my area and would like to take me to dinner. I was thrilled with the prospect. Bill was a man I had dated a few times in Texas, and I always enjoyed his company . . . not to mention his tall, handsome looks and stylish grooming. He was great fun to be with and a gentleman.

During the afternoon of the day Bill and I were to go out, I was riding along in Marilyn's car on the way to my house after we picked up her daughter from school. When I mentioned my *big evening*, she asked what I was planning to wear. "Well, I don't know . . . I really haven't thought about it. What do you think?" She liked the pantsuit I had on and suggested I wear that, but we both noticed a little spot on the front of the jacket; it really needed cleaning before it could be worn again. Marilyn said, "Oh well, you'll find something else, I'm sure," and turned onto my street to drop me off.

"Wait a minute, Mar," I said. "Take me to the cleaners. I want to wear this, and if I don't get it there right now I can't have one-hour service." She stopped the car, looked at me, and inquired, "What will you wear home, Luci? You don't have to wear that outfit tonight, you know."

"Oh yes, I do. Please . . . just drive me to the cleaners and I'll take this off in the car and go home in my underwear. You'll take it in for me, won't you, and protect me from being seen?"

Immediately, I began to undress—jacket, blouse, slacks. As Marilyn headed for the cleaners, I hunkered down in my panties and bra. Sweet little eleven-year-old Beth just stared at me in horror from the backseat. "Don't worry, honey," I assured her, "your mother won't let me be seen in my underwear. It's all right."

When we got to the cleaners' parking lot, I offered a silent prayer of thanks when I saw there was no one else there. Marilyn took my clothes, opened the door, and *left it wide open* as she proceeded into the cleaners to request one-hour service on my behalf. I scrambled to hide behind my purse, a box of Kleenex, and the steering wheel as another car pulled in, and Beth slithered to the floorboard for cover.

When Marilyn got back in the car I choked on a half-hysterical giggle. "Marilyn . . . how could you leave that door open? What if a church member had driven up, or somebody who craved my body? What would I have done?"

In mock innocence she said, "I left the door open? How careless of me."

All the way home we laughed ourselves silly: she, from an upright position behind the steering wheel; I, hunched over with my head in my purse; and Beth, muttering from the backseat floorboard, "I don't believe this . . . I just don't believe it."

From inside my house, Marilyn brought me an old beat-up housecoat that I wouldn't wear to dump the garbage, much less in front of my apartment. But what could I do? I threw the robe on and marched up my walkway like that housecoat was what I always wore to pick up Beth from school. Even now, in the recesses of my mind, I can still hear Marilyn's cackling laughter as she sped away and see Beth's head through the back window, shaking from side to side in perpetual incredulity.

Is there a moral to this crazy story? I think there is—an important one. Some of us are so set in concrete, we can't remember when we last laughed. Or created anything to laugh at. Everything is terribly serious. Heavy. Solemn. I'm not saying there's no place for this kind of attitude . . . but every minute of the day? Where is the joy? Where is the zaniness?

I dare you to do something today that will make you giggle. Invent it yourself. Bend a little. Dare to embrace something a bit risky and wild. And don't put it off until tomorrow. How do you know tomorrow will ever get here?

—*Joy Breaks*

Top Twenty Things
· martha bolton ·

Top Twenty Things You Might Have Been Looking for
When You Couldn't Remember What You Were Looking for:

1. Checkbook
2. Sweater
3. Glasses
4. Paper
5. Pen
6. Wallet
7. Magazine
8. Address book
9. Tape
10. Cell phone
11. Medicine
12. Towel
13. Candy
14. Purse
15. Calculator
16. Shoes
17. Paper clip
18. Husband
19. Pet
20. The right house

—*Cooking with Hot Flashes*

My Secret Diary—I Want to Be a Cover Boy

· mark lowry ·

January 1996

Dear Diary:

Being a big-shot artist, I think it's time I was on the cover of a magazine. Getting on the cover of one of the big-shot Christian music magazines is the ultimate goal for all of us artists. And I've NEVER been on one.

Macho Moped offered me a cover once. But we couldn't agree on the terms. I wanted some sort of payment. So did they.

Buffet Weekly offered me a cover too. The picture was going to be of me at an all-you-can-eat buffet. But it didn't work out. The photographer got tired of constantly having to restock the serving table for the shot.

And I don't like to brag, but *Field & Stream* did offer me a centerfold.

But I still haven't made the cover of a Christian music magazine.

Since, as you know, Diary, I write articles for *Release Magazine*, I figured it was my best chance. It's the least you think the magazine could do after all the award-winning columns I've written for them. (Mama gives out the best awards.)

So, let me tell you what happened today. I was talking on the phone with my illustrious editor-in-chief. We were talking about her Christmas vacation, how she had cried all day in airports and airplanes as she winged her way back to Nashville, sad because she had to leave her home in Canada. As she was sobbing and telling this heartrending tale, I thought it might be a good time to hit her up for a cover.

So between sniffs, (my editor, not me), I said as sweetly and sympathetically as I knew how, "So, how about a cover?"

She heaved a sigh and said, "Mark, you know it wouldn't be a problem if we were a monthly magazine."

Well, it obviously wasn't a problem for the Newsboys. They got a cover. (I don't have anything against the Newsboys. They talk a little funny, and some of their costumes make them look like baldheaded baked potatoes, but they're basically good guys.)

And it wasn't a problem for Amy Grant, either. (I can sing about my heartbeat, too. It's a little sluggish from trying to pump all that gravy through, but that doesn't mean it's not worthy of a song.)

But I didn't mention any of that. Instead, I started sniffing myself and whimpered, "I should have a cover. I deserve a cover. I neeeedddd a COVER."

"Maybe next year, Mark—or the year after that," she mumbled.

"No! I want it now!" I insisted. "I'm a BIG star! When I go grocery shopping, people are always coming up to me and asking, 'Do you know what aisle the Twinkies are on?' or 'Can you help me find the Ben and Jerry's?' I'm not a nobody, you know!"

"We realize that, Mark," she said.

"Then, why haven't you offered me a cover?" I demanded.

"Okay, Mark, here's the truth," she confessed. "With the size of your head, we'd have to run a special 'foldout' cover, and frankly, we just don't have the budget."

So much for my best chance. Time to stalk the other magazines. Maybe I'll give *Field & Stream* another call.

—*Out of Control*

Yo Quiero No Discount

· martha bolton ·

I always feared it would happen someday, and there it was—in black and white. All I had done was walk into a Taco Bell in east Tennessee and give my order to the teenager behind the counter.

I wasn't trying to cause any trouble, or pick a fight, or be disruptive in any way. I was just trying to get a couple of tacos and a seven-layer burrito. *That's all.* It was lunch. There was no justification for what the clerk did. He should have handed me my order and let me pay for it, and I would have been on my way. A simple transaction. But *noooo*. This guy had to take it one step further. He had to be confrontational. He had to take it upon himself to ruin my otherwise happy and peaceful day. He had to keep going until he pushed my buttons. All right, *his* button—the one on the cash register *that printed out the words "SENIOR DISCOUNT" on my receipt!*

SENIOR DISCOUNT! I almost dropped my tray! The nerve of that acne-faced troublemaker! Had I not been so hungry, I would have taken him on right then and there. I would have put my tray down, told him to meet me outside, then papercut him to a pulp with my birth certificate! I may have been over forty, but I was a *long* way from a senior citizen discount!

But I calmed down, decided to turn the other wrinkle—I mean, cheek—and forgive him. It was a simple oversight, after all. I went ahead and gave him the benefit of the doubt. It was the right thing to do. And besides, *a 10 percent discount is a 10 percent discount!*

Maybe he had a migraine headache and his vision was temporarily impaired, I reasoned. Or maybe it was Taco Bell's own version of *Candid Camera.* That's what that little video camera above the cash register was all about. Or, what was most likely the case, the young man's finger slipped, causing him to inadvertently hit the senior discount key instead of the coupon key. That had to have been it. Both keys were probably in the same general area. One little slip is all it would have taken.

That would have been the end of it, except I realized I hadn't ordered a drink and had to go back.

"Diet Pepsi, please," I said, watching his every move this time. His finger hit the Diet Pepsi key, then without even getting anywhere near the coupon key, it went straight for the one marked "senior discount." He didn't hesitate for a second. He was confident. He was beyond confident. He didn't even bother to ask my age. If you're in doubt about something, you usually ask first, don't you? Like if you're not sure if someone's pregnant or if she's just put on a few pounds, most people ask before throwing a baby shower. It's the same principle.

But apparently this guy had no doubt. He was so confident I deserved a senior discount, he announced it as he handed me the receipt.

"Here's your drink, ma'am," he said. "And with the senior discount it comes to $1.09."

I didn't have a choice now. I had to stop him before he dug his hole even deeper.

"*Excuse* me," I said, "but I'm not really a senior. I'm not entitled to a discount. In fact, I shouldn't have gotten a discount on my first order, either."

There, I thought to myself, *I've set the record straight. That should make him think twice before giving away Taco Bell's profits to some other undeserving patron.* I smiled, feeling vindicated and proud of myself that I had made the world a safer place for those of us past the forty mark.

"Aw, close enough," he said. "What's a couple of months?"

It had to be the lighting.

—Didn't My Skin Used to Fit?

I'm planning on living forever. So far, so good!

—AUTHOR UNKNOWN

I'm Not Mr. Fix-It!

· joey o'connor ·

*I*n maledom, there are guys who can make, build, or fix anything. These guys are *Men* with a capital *M*. And then, there are guys like me who get lost driving to Home Depot, who can't tell the difference between a wing nut and a walnut, and whose wives refuse to allow them to use power tools out of fear of turning the garage into a body parts shop. These are normal guys, also called *Losers* with a capital *L*.

Like great white sharks, the guys who can build a redwood deck in forty-five minutes or dismantle a semi-truck blindfolded or drill for oil in their backyards are Manly Men who swim at the top of the home improvement food chain.

Normal guys like me hang out at the lower rungs of the food chain, somewhere between single-cell protozoa and mold spores. When I was running around as a kid wearing my six-gun cowboy holster and shooting up the neighborhood, those other guys were wearing their dads' tool belts and building tree houses that are still standing today. Yeah, now they may be able to build anything with their bare hands, but I'm still a crack shot with my cap gun.

Asking me to install, let's say, a sprinkler system is equivalent to asking me to perform brain surgery. My only two marketable home improvement skills are painting and gardening. There's nothing I can't fix with a gallon of spackle. If I'm out of nails, I'll hang pictures with spackle. If the garbage disposal is busted, I'll spackle it. If the roof has a four-foot hole in it, I'll spackle it.

There's nothing in our home that can't be fixed with spackle. Especially when my wife goes away for the weekend. I'm terrible at brushing my girls' hair and making ponytails. So I just spackle 'em. Only have to do their hair once and it's good for the whole weekend.

Not only am I Mr. Spackle, I can mow. *I'm an excellent lawn mower.* I can usually mow my entire lawn without taking out any sprinkler heads.

Unlike yours truly, Manly Men can do just about anything. These guys are also known as Mr. Fix-Its, and my buddy Glen is one of them. Glen is one of those Swiss Family Robinson-type guys: If he ever gets lost in the woods with a butter knife and a roll of kite string, he'll build an entire shopping mall in a month. He has more tools in his garage than McDonnell Douglas and Boeing combined. Glen is so amazing I am tempted to worship at his feet. *But I am not woorrrthy!*

The other day I went over to his house to help him work on a new fence he was building. On previous weekends, Glen had sur-veyed, dug, poured, and built the cinder-block wall that served as the foundation for the fence, which just happened to circumscribe his entire house. Then, he did something called "tonguing and groov-ing" with five-foot sections of cedar board and connected them to perfectly spaced steel poles cemented into the cinder blocks.

It's a well-known labor principle that work always goes faster with two people. That is, two people who know what they're doing. In our case, there was Glen, who knew exactly what he was doing. And me, who was clueless. That meant Glen now had one and one-sixteenth persons working on his fence.

Glen wouldn't let me touch his table saw, which I thought looked real neat. I'd never been that close to a table saw before. The way it was designed, though, didn't make that much sense to me. How was a guy supposed to cut wood with a sharp, round blade? At least a regular saw had a handle on it. When Glen put a stack of cedar onto the table saw, I smirked and thought to myself, *This'll be interesting.*

Then he flipped the switch.

That thing screamed to life like an F-16 bomber doing a flyby.

He scared the living daylights outta me; nearly had a heart attack. Got that itchy sawdust down my shirt too. Now I know why they call those things power tools.

So listen guys, take it from me. Mr. Fix-Its are the result of nature, not nurture. If you don't have it, you don't have it, and no amount of wishing and hoping is going to change that. Just put on your thinking cap and find a way to earn enough money to hire Mr. Fix-It to build you a deck or caulk your bathtub.

—*Women Are Always Right and Men Are Never Wrong*

Bill Gaither's Bugle

· mark lowry ·

I travel part-time with Bill Gaither, who is a legend in contemporary Christian music. You know the guy. He's in the hymnal. He's written songs like, "The King Is Coming," and "Because He Lives," and "He Touched Me."

Yeah, THAT Bill Gaither.

In 1988, out of the blue, he called me on the phone. I didn't know him personally. I don't even know how he got my number.

But I knew Bill Gaither discovered Sandi Patty. He was famous for discovering people.

Bill Gaither discovered Larnelle Harris.

Bill Gaither discovered Carman.

Bill Gaither discovered Steve Green.

Bill even discovered George Beverly Shea.

(Okay, maybe not George Beverly Shea. But he could have.)

The list goes on and on. You know what Bill Gaither does best? He discovers your hidden talents. When he found Sandi Patty, she was a bass. Bill said, "You know, if you hit a few high notes, you might really go somewhere."

And when he found Larnelle Harris, he was white.

When Bill found me, I was hyperactive.

But even Bill can't change everybody.

He asked me if I'd like to audition for the Gaither Vocal Band.

I said, "Does Billy Graham have a quiet time? You bet your sweet bippy."

I didn't mention that I can't read music. I didn't think that was the time to bring it up. And I didn't tell him that I had never sung baritone before. I didn't want to bring that up, either.

I auditioned, and not too much later, he asked me if I'd like to join the group. And singing with Bill and the Vocal Band have been the most exciting years of my life.

When I first joined the group, I thought he must be perfect to have written such great songs.

He's got a big fancy bus. And he owns it because he wrote "He Touched Me."

He's also a bonafide genius because he married Gloria. What would he be without her? A bunch of music with no words, that's what. (They are so in love, too. One night before a concert, I saw Gloria running her fingers through his hair. It was a wonderful romantic moment, until Bill came in and demanded it back.)

In the back of Bill's fancy bus, he's got a bedroom where he and Gloria sleep. While the rest of us are in bunks piled on top of each other, they've got a bedroom. They've got two beds back there, kind of a Ricky-and-Lucy thing going on, but you didn't hear that from me.

On my first trip traveling with them, I'd catch myself sometimes just staring at him, thinking, "I'm traveling with somebody who's in the hymnal right along with Fanny Crosby." And to travel with somebody in the hymnal is incredible because Fanny doesn't get out much these days.

Then, during one of those first trips, Bill said I could sleep back there in the other bed because Gloria wasn't going with us. So I was in one bed, and he was in the other bed. (That's the way we like it, you know.) I had gone to bed first. I woke up about two in the morning and looked over in Bill's bed. I thought he wasn't there, because all I saw was a pile of pillows. Come to find out, Bill Gaither, Mr. He Touched Me, sleeps under pillows. He doesn't sleep under blankets like a normal person. He roots like a dog under a pile of pillows.

I knew he was under there, because I saw his nose peeking

through those pillows. Actually, it wasn't peeking; it was standing out boldly, proudly. And I started staring at his nose, thinking, *That is Bill Gaither's nose.*

Then he moved around a little, getting comfortable. And I saw his hands and his face pop out.

There's perfect Bill Gaither's perfect hands that wrote those great songs, I thought sleepily.

And there was perfect Bill Gaither's perfect lips, the first to ever speak those legendary lyrics. *There's just something about that name*, I added to myself wistfully.

And there's perfect Bill Gaither's perfect nose that's been forming his high notes for over forty years now, I continued on with my dreamy train of thought.

And while I was chugging along with my perfect thoughts, staring at Bill Gaither's perfect nose—

—that nose let me down.

It started snoring. First it was perfect little snorts, nothing to tarnish his image or anything. It was sort of like a pig digging for roots. Then it went on to become the sound of a freight train hitting a bridge at about ninety miles an hour.

And it didn't stop there. It went on to the sound of a 747 nose-diving to find a seat at the Crystal Cathedral from thirty-thousand feet.

Then his head started spinning around and around and spewing green stuff all over the . . .

(Just kidding.)

Actually, I wouldn't even have minded all the noises Bill Gaither's perfect nose was making if he'd kept a rhythm going.

But it didn't stop there. And it didn't stop all night.

After that first time traveling on the Gaither bus, and after all the years since—exciting as they have been—all I've got to say is that

Bill Gaither may have written "The King Is Coming," but folks, when the King does come, you'd better pray Bill isn't asleep.

Because we'll never hear Gabriel blowing his horn if Bill's blowing his.

—*Out of Control*

I See . . . Sorta
· patsy clairmont ·

The last time I ordered new glasses I had no-glare coating put on the lenses. That way, when I'm on a platform speaking, I don't refract light like some kind of Star Wars invader every time I turn my head. That no-glare stuff really works great, but as in most enhancements, there is a side effect—my lenses smudge easily. In fact, I'm constantly viewing life through thumbprints, which eliminates a lot of life's little details like steps, curbs, and hedges.

Besides the threat of being tripped up, I have to crinkle my face to see through the fog (like I need another crop of deep-set lines in my face). But I think the most disturbing aspect of this smudge factor is that everyone else notices my lenses are a smeared mess. It's sort of like the junk I hide under my bed. I know it's there, but I don't want anyone else to view it. People even offer to clean my glasses for me. How embarrassing. Actually, their efforts only seem to rearrange the design of the smudges. The last set looked similar to the streaming-star effect of going to hyper speed on Han Solo's Millennium Falcon. I'm constantly asked, "How do you see through them?" Well, I don't know. I guess I've adjusted to people looking like walking trees.

Tonight I walked into an optometry store and asked the attendants to remove the no-glare treatment. They looked at me as if I had said, "My name is Chewbacca."

The first gal shot a glance at the other and said, "Is it possible to reverse this process?"

The other one shrugged her shoulders, pleading ignorance as she headed toward me. Staring at the glasses perched atop my nose, she quipped, "How do you see through those?" Here we go again. "Let me clean them for you," she offered. I could see that one coming.

Meanwhile, her cohort had chatted with the specialist in the back who said he could only do the reversal if I had bought the glasses from their store, which I hadn't. Out of frustration, the girl handed back my glasses, telling me they wouldn't come clean (surprise, surprise). She recommended I invest in new lenses, which (surprise, surprise) they could do for me for a little less than a Princess Leia face-lift.

I left in my usual fog, promising to return if I could see any way to buy new spectacles. Then I stumbled through the mall wondering how life would look if I stepped out from behind my cumulus clouds.

There are some advantages in not seeing clearly, you know. I mean, even the little I can see clearly in the morning mirror hasn't been all that wonderful. To see clearly could be more of a reality check than I'm ready for. If my house truly came into focus, I might have to do something radical—like vacuum. Not to mention the obligation I'd feel to weed the garden, wash the windows, and polish the silver. Nah, on second thought, who needs new glasses?

—*Overjoyed!*

The Case of Christine Miller

· luci swindoll ·

All I wanted was something to take the chill off. I was in the Cincinnati airport with my dear friend Ann Wright. Feeling rather cold, I suggested, "How 'bout a nice cup of hot chocolate?" We headed toward a little coffee bar I'd spotted when we deplaned.

We moseyed over to the counter and asked the woman for two cups of hot chocolate. With a smile she said, "We don't serve hot chocolate here, ma'am, but right over there you'll find some. Ask for Christine Miller. They're the best."

Now, I heard *nothing* about Christine Miller. But that was exactly what Ann swears she heard. I felt sure the waitress encouraged us to "ask for skim milk." Since my companion was older, wiser, and more experienced, I took her word for it.

Ann found a table for two as I ordered two Christine Millers. "Christine *what?*" was the incredulous response.

"Christine Millers! I understand that's the best hot chocolate. Two please."

Well, you should have seen the blank expression on that poor woman's face. She verbally stumbled around, drew back from the counter, peered underneath in search of something, and finally responded, "I'm sorry, ma'am. All we have is Carnation." I felt sure she thought we had already been drinking somewhere else.

Holding back my laughter, I muttered, "That's fine. I'll take it; no problem," and went to find the perpetrator of this whole mess. There she sat, patiently waiting for her Christine Miller. I hated to tell her she was having a plain old Carnation hot chocolate!

Ann and I have laughed about that for months. We've told it to others with relish. Who cares if clerks in the Cincinnati airport consider us complete idiots? No harm done. The joke was on us. As I've heard Gloria Gaither say, "Don't hear what I say . . . hear what I mean."

Wouldn't that be great? Sometimes, though, our words are of utmost importance. Saying the right thing is crucial.

Last Christmas I was cruising along the Chilean coast, when suddenly we spotted a wrecked ship jutting out of the water, high and dry. The captain informed us this was the *Santa Leonora*, which, on her maiden voyage in 1964, went aground due to a misunderstood command. The captain and the helmsman had been engaged in conversation when they transited "shoal pass." On completion of their talk, the captain simply said, "Alright, pilot." The pilot responded with a full right rudder, causing the ship to veer sharply to starboard and mount the shallows at full speed, where she still rests today. The captain had said a casual "alright," but the pilot had heard the instruction "all right," which meant something very different. The result was deadly.

God speaks to us clearly. He means what he says. When he says he'll provide, we can count on that. When he promises peace, wisdom, strength, or comfort, they are ours. God imparts his word and keeps it. His words matter! I find tremendous comfort in that.

Sit down with a cup of hot chocolate today and enjoy his Word. Try a Christine Miller, alright?

—Overjoyed!

The Moustache-Waxing
Moments of Life

· sheila walsh ·

*H*ave you ever noticed that aging is full of small indignities? I'm not talking about huge affronts or great mountains to scale, but rather the petty little bug bites of life that let us know we are not twenty or thirty or forty anymore. It might be the number of gray hairs that seem to be winning the color battle and now outnumber the rival brown or blonde ones. It could be the annoying fact that your lipstick seems preoccupied with heading north of your lip-line. It might be the mystery that, even if you weigh pretty much what you weighed ten years ago, clothes just don't seem to fit the same way anymore—things have moved and your metabolism no longer does a tango but a very slow waltz! During the spring of 2005, my husband, Barry, and I decided to do something about that.

We purchased an elliptical exercise machine, which the salesman in the sports store assured us was the latest and best thing. It looks like a cross between a treadmill and a bike and even has a place to hold your bottle of water. I asked the salesman if it would also accommodate a large cup of coffee, but he seemed to think I was joking and never answered.

The machine was delivered in a truck, and two guys set it up in the bedroom. As they left, they handed me the manual, which made the Bible seem like a postcard. The bottom line, as far as I could tell after a quick scan, was that unless each session lasted at least forty minutes I would not be burning fat; I would just be getting my heart rate up. I disappeared into my closet and reappeared clad in sweatpants and my Women of Faith T-shirt. I stepped onto the pedals, and the electronic panel in front of me began to ask rather personal questions: How old are you? How much do you weigh? Do you know your fat-burning rate? Did you tithe last month? (I made that one up.)

I began my climb toward health. I programmed it for forty-five minutes and started pedaling. After some time I looked at the timer to discover that I had been on it for four minutes! I was exhausted. I managed to go for twenty and then fell off. As I lay on the carpet it told me that I had burned three hundred and fifty calories and had worked at my fat-burning heart rate for only 1.2 of the 20 grueling minutes! I have the stamina of an earthworm.

Last week I encountered a fresh indignity in the mystical world of aging as I sat in chair fourteen in my usual nail salon having my artificial nails filled. I don't really like having fake nails, but it is viewed by the men in my family as a gift to them. Barry and Christian love to have their backs scratched. They will sit, faces aglow, purring like cats with a bowl of fresh cream as I gently rake my claws up and down their spines. Last Christmas I had the nails removed to let my real nails breathe for a while and was greeted by stunned silence when I returned from the salon.

"What will we do now, Mom?" Christian asked.

"I thought about that!" I responded, jubilantly producing a back-scratcher that I purchased on my way home. Christian was not impressed.

"That won't work," he said.

"It will work," I assured him. "Let me show you how to use it."

So I surrendered and have made peace with the fact that I will probably have to carry these ten beasts until the trumpet sounds.

The salon I frequent is a large one, and on this particular day every chair was taken. One or two women had said hello as I passed their chairs, acknowledging that they had previously attended a Women of Faith event.

As I sat with someone working on my nails and another on my feet, a new employee approached me and asked if I would like to have my eyebrows waxed. I politely declined because the last time I had that procedure done, it removed most of my forehead as well. With all the determination of a terrier, this girl was not going to be left with idle hands and continued in a loud voice, "How about your moustache? Can I wax your moustache?"

"Moustache?" I said. "Moustache!"

I came home, and as I stared in the mirror, I realized that one of the gifts of God is that, as we age and things begin to grow on us, our eyesight begins to fade, too, so we remain blissfully unaware! That evening I asked Christian at dinner if he was aware that his mother had a moustache.

"Of course not, Mom!" he said laughing.

I was relieved—but only for a moment.

"You don't have a moustache, but you do have a big hair growing out of the side of your face," he said. "Actually, you're quite a hairy person."

Barry rebuked *his* son for oversharing.

"I was just kidding about the hairy person bit, but the hair is there, Dad, honestly; look!" he said.

As I sat in the bath later that night reviewing my role as the missing link, something occurred to me—I couldn't wait to tell Marilyn, Luci, Patsy, Mary, Nicole, and Thelma so that we could all enjoy a good laugh together. That's one of the great joys of friendship. We get to share our triumphs and tragedies, the unexpected joys, and the petty indignities of life. As I slathered on a little more lotion than normal that night, I thought of Solomon's words: "Just as lotions and fragrance give sensual delight, a sweet friendship refreshes the soul" (Proverbs 27:9 MSG).

—*Contagious Joy*

Did you hear about the latest government study on aging?
It cost 240 million dollars and provided compelling
evidence that the average American is growing older.

Retro Solutions for the Chronically Cluttered

· karen scalf linamen ·

I unearthed my Rolodex file from the garage a mere ten minutes ago and I *already* feel better.

No, it doesn't contain the phone number of a masseuse. Or a handsome beau. Or even an express chocolate courier service that guarantees delivery within moments of the onset of a craving or your money back.

In fact, it contains no numbers at all. It's empty. But just *seeing* it gives me hope because this simple little office accoutrement, this outdated data-storing widget if you will, is going to revolutionize my entire life.

I bought this particular Rolodex years ago. It's not the little kind that holds business cards. It's the bigger carousel version that spins 2 x 3 cards around in some sort of rotisserie fashion, like the chicken-broasting machine at your grocer's deli. Except better because broasted chicken never saved anyone's life. At least that I know of.

This Rolodex saved mine for an entire year.

Right after I bought it, I started using it to store all my phone numbers. Then addresses. Then emails. Then birthdays and passwords and the combination to my locker at the gym.

Before long I'd added the dates of my last oil change, the name of the video game my kids wanted for Christmas, and the recipe for homemade Play Dough.

Soon I was going through my entire house with a laundry basket, collecting all the weird scraps of paper on which I'd written pertinent information. I found the shoebox lid with the service ID number for my laptop. The table napkin with the birthdays of my niece and nephews. The used envelope on which I'd handwritten detailed directions for reprogramming my VCR.

I wrote the information in my Rolodex and tossed the clutter.

I dug deeper, going through my wallet, sifting through piles on my desk, sorting through shoeboxes filled with heaven-knows-what. I was on a roll now. Dental appointment reminder cards? Gone. The schedule for the coming opera season that I never attend but always think I will? Gone. The salvaged magazine pages I've hung onto for two years because they contain 800-numbers for household gadgets I'm almost pretty sure I can't live without?

All gone.

When I found a slip of paper with directions for patching our inflatable kiddie pool, I wrote the instructions on a Rolodex card and threw that paper—like all the others—in the trash. I even stapled the accompanying patching fabric to the back of the card.

In other words, I stuck *everything* in that Rolodex. Anything just lying around the house was fair game. One day I spotted something I'd missed and made a beeline, but my teenager saw me coming and fled to the mall.

This simple Rolodex kept my house clutter-free for an entire year. Until the day I decided to "upgrade" to a PDA.

After months of technical difficulties, software crashes, and an unending learning curve, I got frustrated. Before long, I'd reverted back to my old ways, hanging onto random papers, writing things down on weird little scraps. Like rising floodwaters, clutter seeped, then poured back into my life.

I've been drowning ever since. Until this morning, when I reclaimed my Old Friend from a box next to the wiper fluid.

I'm coming to the conclusion that newer isn't always better. Old school can still rule. And sometimes the stuff we discarded yesterday is the very thing we still need in our lives today.

See why unearthing this simple desktop gadget is such a big deal? It's not just a Rolodex. It's a way of life.

I'll bet you've never said that about a broasted chicken.

Customer: "So that'll get me connected to the Internet, right?"
Tech Support: "Yeah."
Customer: "And that's the latest version of the Internet, right?"
Tech Support: "Uhh—uh—uh-yeah."

There are 10 types of people in the world: those who
understand binary, and those who don't.

How Things Don't Work

· marilyn meberg ·

When I retired my counseling practice, moved to the desert, and signed a two-book contract with Word Publishing, it seemed clear to those who take a proprietary interest in my well-being that a computer would be a necessity. The prevailing logic was, "Marilyn, once you get the hang of it, and you will very soon, you will be stunned at the amount of time saved by using a computer for your writing."

I have long harbored the suspicion that I could not sleep in a place that also housed a computer. However, when my son, Jeff, and his wife, Carla, began to talk about the advantages of a computer for me, I started to listen. I suppose the clincher was the fact that Carla and I could do battle for who qualifies as more technologically challenged. If Carla could master a computer, then surely there was hope for me.

Under the inspiration of that realization and with the persistently kind advice of many, Pat Wenger volunteered to buy a laptop computer for me. The laptop came equipped to do all I needed and more, should I choose.

Pat made the purchase because I couldn't imagine being in the same room with a bunch of computers, let alone a whole store full of electronic gadgets. Nor would I have the foggiest notion of what questions to ask. Pat feared I might in all innocence and incompetence come home with a digital machine to measure blood pressure.

I will spare you the details of the hours and even days I have lost in my efforts to save time by using a computer, but I would like to say that computers are utterly inexplicable to me. Not only that, but they also have an attitude. At least mine does! For instance, something as simple as closing out a program and shutting down the computer sends the little demonic person who scowlingly sits inside the machine day and night into parental mode. A question flashes on the screen: "Are you sure you want to shut down your machine?" Until the question was asked, I was quite certain I wanted to shut it down, but with those bold words glaring at me, I hesitate. Maybe I was wrong. Does the little machine person know something I don't? Will something irreparable happen if it shuts down? Not wanting to appear uncertain, I click yes. But my self-confidence is undermined, and I wait nervously for the whole thing to explode all over my lap.

Another equally unsettling question the little demon machine person loves to flash on the screen is, "Are you sure you want to do that?" I hate that because I'm not sure about anything. I'd like to say, "Don't ask," but I'm too intimidated. Instead, I find myself talking aloud to the screen in an effort to justify my thinking.

The most judgmental action the computer has ever taken with me occurred when, in utter disgust and frustration, I typed in an accusatory word that I must admit I would not use in polite society. However, I felt it was appropriate for the demonic little person who had been second-guessing, bossing, and not cooperating with me all morning. The minute I typed in my retort, the screen went blank, but not before telling me it would not tolerate my word.

As long as I'm venting, let me say I find computer terminology utterly illogical. For instance, why on earth is a paper copy called "hard copy"? It isn't hard at all. On the other hand a "floppy disk" is as unpliable as the character living in my computer. Why not call a paper copy "floppy" and a disk "hard"? Now isn't that logical?

I had the audacity to express these thoughts one evening to a group of computer literates (one of my more boring evenings) and received lofty, patronizing statements like, "It's really not all that difficult."

As long as we're talking computer absurdities, can anyone tell me why on earth the pointer is called a mouse? For goodness sake, a mouse is a rodent! I can't imagine anything more repellent than having daily hand contact with something called a mouse. If we have to have an image of something small and furry that illogically represents a pointer, why not call it a canary? At least they're appealing. Good grief! I've worked myself into a frenzy. Better go rest my brain.

—*I'd Rather Be Laughing*

Protect me from knowing what I don't need to know.
Protect me from even knowing that there are things to
know that I don't know.
Protect me from knowing that I decided not to know about
the things that I decided not to know about.
Amen.

Lord, protect me from the consequences
of the above prayer.

—DOUGLAS ADAMS

Oops, I've Fallen

· patsy clairmont ·

We definitely live in a fallen world. Why, just today I was attacked by a doll. Not just any doll but one of my own. I had her standing on my dresser top, and when I bent over to slide open a drawer, she fell and beaned me on my noggin. Her head is porcelain while mine, I thought, was granite. Evidently my noodle is more the consistency of Silly Putty, because her head left a crater-sized indentation in my cranium. She came down with such a thud it took me several minutes before I could carry on.

Speaking of noodles, get this. In Japan a noodle museum is all the rage. Honest. It's far more popular than the art museums, which are generally visited only by scholars.

Imagine if someone could combine the two. The "Mona Lisa" could be done in rigatoni (be hard for her not to smirk). Or picture "Whistler's Mother" trying to rock on a chair of macaroni. (Next we'll be sticking a feathered hat on her.) Or how about "The Girl with the Watering Can" being renamed "The Girl with the Ravioli."

Actually, the noodle museum is dedicated to the ramen noodle, which I understand is as popular in Japan as hot dogs are in Chicago's O'Hare Airport (more are sold there than anywhere else in the country). In one year the Japanese wolf down enough noodles at the museum's nine ramen shops to encircle the globe five times. Wow! Imagine if it rained. It could give new meaning to "wet noodle"—although if it filled in the ozone hole that could be good.

I think the news proves daily how off our noodles we humans are. Our fallen condition is proclaimed continuously by our odd behavior. I think of individuals who have been featured on the ten o'clock news for scaling high-rise buildings in major cities. The

Andes are one thing, but the Empire State Building? C'mon, what's that about? Or skydiving off the Space Needle. Spacey, if you ask me. But then, truth be known, I've done a few weird things myself.

I remember the time I wound my foot around my neck (I was much younger) in an attempt to duplicate a trick by a TV contortionist. I managed to slide my foot around the back of my neck, but when my toes hooked close to my ear, I couldn't unwind myself. It took just seconds to realize what an unnatural position this was, so I yelled to my husband for help.

To suggest Les was amazed when he tromped into the room and saw his wife in a virtual knot would be to underestimate his incredulous response. "Hurry," I commanded, hoping to jolt him into action. It worked, and he dislodged my foot, releasing the pressure off my cramping leg. I appreciated his assistance but was a tad irritated at his incessant snickering during the unwinding process.

Of course, I remember the time Les fell two stories off a roof with two bundles of roofing tiles on his shoulder. Falling off a roof is not odd. What was odd was when he stood up after several moments of staring at the sky, picked up the bundles, and scaled his way back up to the roof to finish the job.

If it isn't dolls falling on us and knocking us silly, our own silly fascinations remind us that sometimes we let life get out of whack. All that points to our fallen nature. We just can't keep things in balance (or balanced on our dresser tops).

When in doubt about your need to be saved, just check what's out of place in your life. It could be decorations that don't stay put, interests that become fetishes, or some less-than-bright action you've taken. Fortunately, even if something falls on our noodle or if we fall on our behind, God's everlasting arms pick us up, and he embraces us with his loving-kindness.

—*Overjoyed!*

One thing I've noticed about getting older, my memory isn't as sharp as it used to be. Also, my memory isn't as sharp as it used to be.

You know you're getting older when you lean over to pick something up off the floor and ask yourself if there's something else you need to do while you're down there.

Actual Newspaper Headlines

(With a Little Slip of the Tongue)

- Grandmother of Eight Makes Hole in One
- Deaf Mute Gets New Hearing in Killing
- Police Begin Campaign to Run Down Jaywalkers
- House Passes Gas Tax on to Senate
- Stiff Opposition Expected to Casketless Funeral Plan
- Two Convicts Evade Noose, Jury Hung
- William Kelly Was Fed Secretary
- Milk Drinkers Are Turning to Powder
- Safety Experts Say School Bus Passengers Should Be Belted
- Quarter of a Million Chinese Live on Water
- Farmer Bill Dies in House
- Iraqi Head Seeks Arms

Eating Advice

· mark lowry ·

I love to eat. My favorite food is Mexican food. I was raised in Texas, and Texas has the best Mexican food in the world. Texas has better Mexican food than Mexico does.

But when you're in Texas and you're looking for a good place to eat Mexican food, never ask a skinny person. Skinny people are no fun. They're usually miserable. You know why? Because they're hungry! Fat people are more fun, and they always know the best places to eat.

I spoke at a banquet not long ago. The group was great, but the food stunk. They fed us a steak, a baked potato, a salad, and some sort of moon-shaped, orange-colored vegetable they placed right between the steak and potato. I had never seen a moon-shaped orange-colored vegetable in my life. So I bit into it, and I'm here to tell you, it was nasty! It sort of crunched, and it had *no* flavor.

I asked them what it was.

"Sweet potato," they informed me.

"Sweet potatoes aren't supposed to crunch," I told them. "Doritos are supposed to crunch. Sweet potatoes are supposed to come out of the oven on Thanksgiving morning with marshmallows on top of them and some unknown liquor substance my Mama sneaks into the house at Christmastime over them."

"Oh, but it's healthier this way," they explained.

Healthier, huh? That is the stupidest thing I've ever heard. In my opinion, vegetables were not meant to crunch. Broccoli, for instance. It's not supposed to be crunchy; it's supposed to be cooked so long it almost turns yellow. Then it's supposed to have cheese sauce poured all over it to disguise the ugly yellow color.

I was up north once and got into a discussion about food with a pitifully healthy-looking lady. "Oh, we don't overcook our vegetables up here," she said. "We don't want to cook the vitamins out of the vegetables."

"For goodness' sakes," I told her, "take a pill and cook the vegetables!" You ever bite into a vitamin pill? They taste awful. You know why? Because they've got vitamins in them. That's why you need to cook those vitamins right out of those vegetables. They'll taste better. Forget the health nuts. We're all gonna be dead in a hundred years, for goodness' sakes. *Cook the vegetables!*

Fatty, greasy, crunchy, you fry it, I love it. I want my blood going through my veins saying, "Excuse me, pardon me, coming through, pardon me."

I want mashed potatoes with a lake of gravy in 'em. And leave the skin on the chicken. Don't make that bird die in vain—fry that chicken!

Put the sugar in the tea; that's where it goes. Not that pink stuff that causes cancer. I like my tea so sweet that if I run out of syrup, I can pour it over my pancakes.

And then, whatever you do, don't exercise all those fine calories off! Like I said, I do one sit-up a day. I get up in the morning. That's half. I lie down at night. That's the other half.

I figured out a long time ago, my body is for nothing more than carrying my head from place to place anyway.

—*Out of Control*

Gray hair is God's graffiti.

—BILL COSBY

If your mind is going fuzzy and you find that you can't
remember someone's name, try this trick. With a smile on
your face to hide the confusion, say, "Now you are?"
Let's say the young woman before you answers, "Mary."
Then you respond with, "Of course, I know you're Mary.
It's your last name I've forgotten."
This works really well . . .
unless Mary happens to be your daughter.

Acknowledgments

Grateful acknowledgment is made to the publishers and copyright holders who granted permission to reprint copyrighted material.

Part I. I've Never Seen Those Kids Before in My Life!

"High Drama at the Bank" by Carol Kent, taken from *Detours, Tow Trucks, and Angels in Disguise*. Colorado Springs, Colorado: NavPress, 1996. (www.navpress.com). Used by permission. All rights reserved.

"Okay You Guys" by Kathy Peel, taken from *Do Plastic Surgeons Take VISA?* Nashville, Tennessee: Word Publishing, 1992. All rights reserved.

"They're Out to Rule the World" by Martha Bolton, taken from *Cooking with Hot Flashes*. Minneapolis, Minnesota: Bethany House, a Division of Baker Publishing Group, 2004. Used by permission. All rights reserved.

"K. C. and the Ark" by Carol Kent, taken from *Detours, Tow Trucks, and Angels in Disguise*. Colorado Springs, Colorado: NavPress, 1996. (www.navpress.com). Used by permission. All rights reserved.

"College-Bound Kids Empty Our Nest" by Marti Attoun. Used by permission of the author. All rights reserved.

"You Rile the Kids Up, You Put 'Em to Bed" by Joey O'Connor, taken from *Women Are Always Right and Men Are Never Wrong*. Nashville, Tennessee: Word Publishing, 1998. Used by permission. All rights reserved.

"With Friends Like These" by Luci Swindoll, taken from *Joy Breaks*. Nashville, Tennessee: Women of Faith, Inc., 1997. Used by permission. All rights reserved.

"You Know There's a Baby in the House When ..." by Martha Bolton, taken from *Who Put the Pizza in the VCR?* Published by Servant Publications, 1996. Used by permission of the author. All rights reserved.

"A Parent's Guide to Souvenir Shopping" by Marti Attoun. Used by permission of the author. All rights reserved.

Part II. Say Goodnight, Gracie!

"Poor Ruth" by Sheila Walsh, taken from *I'm Not Wonder Woman but God Made Me Wonderful.* Nashville, Tennessee: Thomas Nelson, Inc., 2006. Used by permission. All rights reserved.

"Risky Business" by Patsy Clairmont, taken from *Normal Is Just a Setting on Your Dryer.* Wheaton, Illinois: Tyndale House Publishers, 1993. Used by permission of the author. All rights reserved.

"The Rules" by Joey O'Connor, taken from *Women Are Always Right and Men Are Never Wrong.* Nashville, Tennessee: Word Publishing, 1998. Used by permission. All rights reserved.

"A Dumpster So Divine" by Marti Attoun. Used by permission of the author. All rights reserved.

"Are You Finished with That?" by Sheila Walsh, taken from *Overjoyed.* Nashville, Tennessee: Women of Faith, Inc., 1999. Used by permission. All rights reserved.

"Husband for Sale" by Carol Kent, taken from *Detours, Tow Trucks, and Angels in Disguise.* Colorado Springs, Colorado: NavPress, 1996. (www.navpress.com). Used by permission. All rights reserved.

"Not Another One of Those Parties!" by Joey O'Connor, taken from *Women Are Always Right and Men Are Never Wrong.* Nashville, Tennessee: Word Publishing, 1998. Used by permission. All rights reserved.

"You've Got Male" by Anita Renfroe, taken from *Purse-Driven Life.* Colorado Springs, Colorado: NavPress, 1996. (www.navpress.com). Used by permission. All rights reserved.

"Messages" by Patsy Clairmont, taken from *God Uses Cracked Pots.*

Wheaton, Illinois: Tyndale House Publishers, 1993. Used by permission of the author. All rights reserved.

"You Should Know How I Feel" by Joey O'Connor, taken from *Women Are Always Right and Men Are Never Wrong*. Nashville, Tennessee: Word Publishing, 1998. Used by permission of the author. All rights reserved.

"Up and Adam" by Todd and Jedd Hafer, taken from *Snickers from the Front Pew*. Published by Honor Books, 2000. Used by permission of the authors. All rights reserved.

Part III. Dogs, Cats, and Caribou!

"Help, Lord, There's a Cat on My Face" by Sheila Walsh, taken from *Overjoyed*. Nashville, Tennessee: Women of Faith, Inc., 1999. Used by permission. All rights reserved.

"Princess Fur-Face" by Marilyn Meberg, taken from *Extravagant Joy*. Nashville, Tennessee: Women of Faith, Inc., 2000. Used by permission. All rights reserved.

"In the Company of Critters" by Karen Linamen, taken from *Welcome to the Funny Farm*. Grand Rapids, Michigan: Revell Books, a Division of Baker Publishing Group. Used by permission. All rights reserved.

"Developing 'Sponsibility" by Marilyn Meberg, taken from *I'd Rather Be Laughing*. Nashville, Tennessee: W Publishing Group, a Division of Thomas Nelson, Inc., 1998. Used by permission. All rights reserved.

"Don't Make Eye Contact" by Patsy Clairmont, taken from *I Second that Emotion*. Nashville, Tennessee: Thomas Nelson, Inc., 2008. Used by permission. All rights reserved.

"Cody the Canine Crackup" by Patsy Clairmont, taken from *All Cracked Up*. Nashville, Tennessee: W Publishing Group, a Division of Thomas Nelson, Inc., 2006. Used by permission. All rights reserved.

Part IV. Giggling in the Pews

"Todd Wields the Sword: His Own Story" by Todd Hafer, taken from *Snickers from the Front Pew*. Published by Honor Books, 2000. Used by permission of the author. All rights reserved.

"Potlucks: Not Always Good Fortune" by Todd and Jedd Hafer, taken from *Snickers from the Front Pew*. Published by Honor Books, 2000. Used by permission of the authors. All rights reserved.

"Just Say Thanks" by Mark Lowry, taken from *Out of Control*. Nashville, Tennessee: Word Publishing, 1996. Used by permission. All rights reserved.

"The Glory of Gum" by Marti Attoun. Used by permission of the author. All rights reserved.

"Adventures at Church Camp" by Mark Lowry, taken from *Out of Control*. Nashville, Tennessee: Word Publishing, 1996. Used by permission. All rights reserved.

"Church Basketball: Throwing Up a Prayer" by Todd and Jedd Hafer, taken from *Snickers from the Front Pew*. Published by Honor Books, 2000. Used by permission of the authors. All rights reserved.

Part V. On the Road and in the Air

"Accidental Perspective" by Patsy Clairmont, taken from *Normal Is Just a Setting on Your Dryer*. Wheaton, Illinois: Tyndale House Publishers, 1993. Used by permission of the author. All rights reserved.

"Location, Location, Location" by Mark Lowry, taken from *Out of Control*. Nashville, Tennessee: Word Publishing, 1996. Used by permission. All rights reserved.

"The Joys of Business Travel" by Kathy Peel, taken from *Do Plastic Surgeons Take VISA?* Nashville, Tennessee: Word Publishing, 1992. All rights reserved.

"Another Town, Another Trauma" by Sheila Walsh, taken from

Overjoyed. Nashville, Tennessee: Women of Faith, Inc., 1999.
Used by permission. All rights reserved.

"Where's Your Drive" by Martha Bolton, taken from *Didn't My Skin Used to Fit?* Minneapolis, Minnesota: Bethany House, a Division of Baker Publishing Group. Used by permission. All rights reserved.

"Hurry Up, We're Going to Be Late" by Joey O'Connor, taken from *Women Are Always Right and Men Are Never Wrong.* Nashville, Tennessee: Word Publishing, 1998. Used by permission. All rights reserved.

"Driving Advice" by Mark Lowry, taken from *Out of Control.* Nashville, Tennessee: Word Publishing, 1996. Used by permission. All rights reserved.

"Murphy's Laws of Driving" by Joe Hickman, taken from www.HaLife.com. Used by permission of the author. All rights reserved.

"Life with Momo" by Luci Swindoll, taken from *Life, Celebrate It!* Nashville, Tennessee: W Publishing Group, a Division of Thomas Nelson, Inc., 2006. Used by permission. All rights reserved.

"Church Van (Unsafe at Any Speed)" by Todd and Jedd Hafer, taken from *Snickers from the Front Pew.* Published by Honor Books, 2000. Used by permission of the authors. All rights reserved.

Part VI. A Mind Is a Terrible Thing to Waste!

"Crafty" by Patsy Clairmont, taken from *Normal Is Just a Setting on Your Dryer.* Wheaton, Illinois: Tyndale House Publishers, 1993. Used by permission of the author. All rights reserved.

"My Olympic Suggestions" by Andy Andrews. www.andyandrews.com. Used by permission of the author. All rights reserved.

"Rats Giggle" by Marilyn Meberg, taken from *Overjoyed.* Nashville, Tennessee: Women of Faith, Inc., 1999. Used by permission. All rights reserved.

"Most Dedicated to the Task" by Patsy Clairmont, taken from *Normal Is Just a Setting on Your Dryer*. Wheaton, Illinois: Tyndale House Publishers, 1993. Used by permission of the author. All rights reserved.

"You're as Young as You're Ever Gonna Be" by Anita Renfroe, taken from *Purse-Driven Life*. Colorado Springs, Colorado: NavPress, 1996. (www.navpress.com). Used by permission. All rights reserved.

"Lord, Did You Misunderstand?" by Natalie Grant, taken from *The Real Me*. Nashville, Tennessee: W Publishing, a Division of Thomas Nelson, Inc., 2005. Used by permission. All rights reserved.

"Hair Today, Gone Tomorrow" by Sheila Walsh, taken from *Overjoyed*. Nashville, Tennessee: Women of Faith, Inc., 1999. Used by permission. All rights reserved.

"I Dare You" by Luci Swindoll, taken from *Joy Breaks*. Nashville, Tennessee: Women of Faith, Inc., 1997. Used by permission. All rights reserved.

"Top Twenty Things" by Martha Bolton, taken from *Cooking with Hot Flashes*. Minneapolis, Minnesota: Bethany House, a Division of Baker Publishing Group. Used by permission. All rights reserved.

"My Secret Diary—I Want to Be a Cover Boy" by Mark Lowry, taken from *Out of Control*. Nashville, Tennessee: Word Publishing, 1996. Used by permission. All rights reserved.

"Yo Quiero No Discount" by Martha Bolton, taken from *Didn't My Skin Used to Fit?* Minneapolis, Minnesota: Bethany House, a Division of Baker Publishing Group. Used by permission. All rights reserved.

"I'm Not Mr. Fix-It!" by Joey O'Connor, taken from *Women Are Always Right and Men Are Never Wrong*. Nashville, Tennessee: Word Publishing, 1998. Used by permission. All rights reserved.

"Bill Gaither's Bugle" by Mark Lowry, taken from *Out of Control.* Nashville, Tennessee: Word Publishing, 1996. Used by permission. All rights reserved.

"I See . . . Sorta" by Patsy Clairmont, taken from *Overjoyed.* Nashville, Tennessee: Women of Faith, Inc., 1999. Used by permission. All rights reserved.

"The Case of Christine Miller" by Luci Swindoll, taken from *Overjoyed.* Nashville, Tennessee: Women of Faith, Inc., 1999. Used by permission. All rights reserved.

"The Moustache-Waxing Moments of Life" by Sheila Walsh, taken from *Contagious Joy.* Nashville, Tennessee: W Publishing Group, a Division of Thomas Nelson, Inc., 2006. Used by permission. All rights reserved.

"Retro Solutions for the Chronically Cluttered" by Karen Linamen. Used by permission of the author. All rights reserved.

"How Things Don't Work" by Marilyn Meberg, taken from *I'd Rather Be Laughing.* Nashville, Tennessee: W Publishing Group, a Division of Thomas Nelson, Inc. 1998. Used by permission. All rights reserved.

"Oops, I've Fallen" by Patsy Clairmont, taken from *Overjoyed.* Nashville, Tennessee: Women of Faith, Inc., 1999. Used by permission. All rights reserved.

"Eating Advice" by Mark Lowry, taken from *Out of Control.* Nashville, Tennessee: Word Publishing, 1996. Used by permission. All rights reserved.

Scripture-Inspired Thoughts to Bless Your Day, Every Day

Wake up! It's time to start your day with the amazing ladies from Women of Faith. Or hey, if you're a night owl there's no better way to finish your day. Either way, you now have a dose of love and wisdom for every day of the year.

THOMAS NELSON
Since 1798

WOMEN OF FAITH

womenoffaith.com

WOMEN OF FAITH®

womenoffaith.com
Encouraging Women Every Day

What's New
Keep up with what's going on at
Women of Faith

Upcoming Events
Videos, schedules, things to do in
event cities, and more

Online Registration
Choose your seat with our interactive
arena maps and sign up

Shop
A huge collection of products just
waiting for you

Faith to Faith e-News
Sign up for our FREE monthly
newsletter

Book Club
Exclusive interviews, excerpts, and a
25% discount on the featured book